High Flight

High Flight

The Life and Poetry of Pilot Officer John Gillespie Magee

Roger Cole

First published in hardback in 2013 by Fighting High Ltd
www.fightinghigh.com

Copyright © Fighting High Ltd, 2013
Copyright text © Roger Cole, 2013

This paperback edition first published 2020

British Library Cataloguing-in-Publication data.
A CIP record for this title is available from the
British Library.

Paperback ISBN – 13: 978-1838068707
ebook ISBN – 13: 978-0993415241
Hardback ISBN – 13: 9780957116368

Designed and typeset by Michael Lindley
www.truthstudio.co.uk

Printed and bound by Gomer Press
Front cover design by Michael Lindley

High Flight

Oh! I have slipped the surly bonds of Earth
And danced the skies on laughter-silvered wings;
Sunward I've climbed, and joined the tumbling mirth
of sun-split clouds, — and done a hundred things
You have not dreamed of — wheeled and soared and swung
High in the sunlit silence. Hov'ring there,
I've chased the shouting wind along, and flung
My eager craft through footless halls of air . . . .

Up, up the long, delirious, burning blue
I've topped the wind-swept heights with easy grace.
Where never lark, or even eagle flew —
And, while with silent, lifting mind I've trod
The high untrespassed sanctity of space,
Put out my hand, and touched the face of God.

Contents

Foreword

by The Reverend Canon F. Hugh Magee

Roger Cole has kindly asked me to contribute a foreword to his biography of my late brother, John Gillespie Magee Jnr. As John's only surviving brother, I am glad to do so.

It is some years since a new biography of John has appeared, and Roger Cole's extensively researched memoir is a welcome addition to the corpus. There is much new material here, and it is particularly gratifying to have such a detailed narrative of John's career as a pilot, much of it related in his own words. It is also inspiring to have this detailed account of the friendships that John formed, both at Rugby School and during his final days as an accomplished pilot officer in the Royal Canadian Air Force.

I am struck as well by the fact that Roger has begun his work with a fitting tribute to Leading Aircraftman Ernest Aubrey Griffin, who died with John in their mid-air collision over Lincolnshire in 1941. I recall visiting Ernest Griffin's parents in Oxford with my mother after the war. As one might expect, the news of John's death was a real shock to all of us who knew him. But I think it is fair to say that its impact on his immediate family was greatly eased by the fact that our parents simply did not accept death as anything more than a moment of transition. In breaking the news to me my mother simply explained that my brother John had 'gone to be with our heavenly Father'. Having been brought up in a genuinely Christian family, I did not find this difficult to accept, though I of course knew that, along with my brothers, I would miss John terribly.

As a kind of footnote to the drama of that moment, my mother, who was a deeply spiritual person, liked to recall an experience she had shortly after receiving the news. It so happened that she needed to leave the house soon after to do an errand in the neighbourhood of Washington DC, where we were living at the time. She said later that she was totally convinced that John was with her as she went on her way. From her account, John communicated with her directly, telling her that all was well.

Well, I myself cannot claim to have had such a supernatural experience of John's presence after his death. In fact, I was only 8 when he died in 1941, and my memories of him are therefore not extensive. But, few as they are, those memories remain fresh in my mind.

Two of them particularly stand out, not least because it has not been difficult for me to associate these recollections with emotions John expressed in the poem for which he is best known, 'High Flight'.

The first had to do with John's willingness to connive with me in a little practical joke. As described by Roger Cole in his memoir, John, during what was to be his final leave prior to embarkation to Britain in 1941, enjoyed driving the family for outings into the countryside around Washington in the enormous Packard convertible he had bought second-hand the previous summer.

One of these outings found us heading towards a swimming pool made available to us for the occasion by the day camp in Maryland that I attended after school in those days. Having been to this secluded spot a number of times, I was aware of the fact that there were some dips in the road that led to it. So I knew that, if one was travelling at a decent speed, those sitting in the back seat of a car were likely to get unexpectedly tossed into the air (this was before the advent of seat belts), an effect obviously heightened if the car happened to be a convertible! Shortly before we arrived at this stretch of road, I insisted that we stop and that the family be rearranged in such a way as to provide the maximum airborne surprise to the maximum number of family members. John was immediately up for this joke and obligingly drove along the relevant stretch of road at maximum speed, so humouring his youngest brother and, no doubt, his own daredevil spirit!

The other episode that stands out in my mind is something I will never forget. The Packard referred to above was preceded by a more modest Ford (I remember it from its rumble seat!). At the time (the summer of 1940), and as Roger relates, the family had taken a holiday home in the town of Oak Bluffs on Martha's Vineyard, off the coast of Massachusetts. Mail had to be picked up every day from the main post office, and, since our house was located on the outskirts, one of John's daily tasks, as the only member of the family with a driver's licence, was to retrieve the mail. On one such occasion John took me along. It was a precious time alone with him. On the way home, while driving along a coastal highway by the harbour (the road is still there), John suddenly pressed the accelerator to the floor so as to push the engine to its limit – he 'gunned it', in other words. He then proceeded to shout at the top of his lungs! It was a thrilling, exhilarating moment for both of us.

These two episodes, especially the latter one, have always seemed to me to reflect something of that spirit of exultation that one finds expressed in two lines of 'High Flight':

> I've chased the shouting wind along, and flung
> My eager craft through footless halls of air. . .

Be that as it may, my memories of John, though precious few, remain with me, and I feel close to him to this day.

Happily, I likewise feel a sense of that same closeness to John through what Roger Cole has now written about him some seventy years later, and I am grateful to Roger for having made the effort.

Preface

I moved to live in the village of Wellingore in Lincolnshire in 1971. I knew little of its past history, but gradually over the years different aspects of its near and distant past became known to me through my own researches and the memories of other residents. Some had family connections in the immediate locality going back several generations and I was fascinated to be able to piece together details of the past from photographs, maps, letters, drawings and personal recollections. This then led me to explore the papers related to the village held in the Lincolnshire Archive and Lincoln Cathedral Library.

In 1970 the most imposing building in the village was Wellingore Hall, standing adjacent to the church. When I enquired about its dilapidated condition, it was explained that it had never recovered from the use it had been put to during the Second World War.

The Hall and its grounds had served as a Mess for hundreds of men and women who serviced and flew from Wellingore airfield and the many others located nearby.

It also gradually became apparent from visitors who came to the village that many of them had travelled from as far away as America and Canada to find where lost loved ones had spent the last months of their lives. From their questions, many of which could not be answered, I determined to try to piece together this almost forgotten history of the village during the years of the Second World War.

Certain names, some famous and known to me, recurred in the answers to my questions, and then one day I was confronted by a Canadian visitor who asked me to show him where the famous author of the poem 'High Flight' had been billeted. I had no idea whom he was referring to and so decided to find out who this poet was and how and when he had come to live in the village. Once I had begun to shape my researches, answers and explanations came from many sources. Some provided conflicting evidence, while others, often in casual comments, offered amazing insights into the military occupation of those undocumented years.

In the middle of my research I became friends with David and Caroline Chrisp, who lived in a house near the church called The Grange. Adjacent to Wellingore Hall, it too had been used as an Officers' Mess during the war and still carried the scars of burnt-out cigarette stubs on its wooden floors. David and Caroline then introduced me to Ivan Henson from Gloucestershire, who had visited them on several occasions in his quest to find out about John Magee. He, like me, shared a fascination about the life and poetry of John Magee.

Our meeting came at an opportune moment when I was searching for the details to substantiate my explorations and he was looking for someone to help him to construct the chronology for his researches in order to write a book. Unfortunately Ivan died before the task was completed. But, with the gift to me of his research papers by his brother Tony, I moved one step closer to achieving our shared ambition to publish an account of the life and achievements of this brilliant young man. The book describes a man who through his unique use of language expressed the thoughts and ideals of all who share a fascination with flight. Thanks then to Ivan. I am sure he would be proud of this story.

My research for this book became a total preoccupation. At first it seemed that everything I wished to know and the documents I wanted to read were thousands of miles away in America, Canada or even China. Even the documents in England were difficult to locate. So, as with all research, one small piece of evidence led to another, and I gradually found that some of the people whom I wanted to meet and talk to from the past were in fact alive and only too willing to tell their story. On the one hand, a nurse who had looked after John for only a few days in a military hospital in Wales in 1939. On the other hand, Elinor, who sustained the longest, closest and most important friendship of his life.

It was Elinor who provided the idea of the way this book might be written. As we sat in front of the fire in her little hillside cottage in Wales, she simply said, 'I can hear his words now as if he were with us, you should write about him like he is with us now . . . you should let his words and mine and anyone else you can meet who loved him like we all did, tell the story for you.' So that is how the years of meetings with the people who informed my researches have come together in this text. It is not my intention to give the impression that I was present when these intimate and important incidents in his life occurred. Rather it is to give the reader a unique insight into the experiences and conversations, beliefs, loves and despairs, that shaped this incredible young poet and pilot.

I have simply selected cameos from the hundreds of stories about John that have been shared with me by people from all over the world. I have chosen to select and represent them in a particular order, and only time and space have determined how many have found their place in this final selection.

Acknowledgements

I am grateful to Hugh Magee, John's brother. He was christened Frederick Hugh, but all his family know him today as Hugh. He has been very generous to me, and I have shared the development of this book with him by reading aloud parts of different chapters during their preparation. His support has provided me with an enabling strength of purpose. The endorsement of his Foreword gives the book a sense of completeness.

I am also indebted to my brother-in-law Malcolm Rowson for his patience and perseverance with me as I struggled to manage the complex technologies of the computer age. He provided not only technical support but a professional evaluation of the writing, and accompanied me on some of the more unusual interviews and excursions that informed the text.

I hope that the aspects of John's life that inspired me to bring these chapters together will provide others with an insight into the values, purposes and beliefs of this exceptional young man.

We do not need to surmise as to what John might have achieved but celebrate and be thankful for what he did! Thank you to all of you, both those living now and others sadly deceased, for helping me to create this unique record of the life and work of John Magee.

(Publisher's note: We would like to express our appreciation to Linda Granfield for her assistance with the picture section captions.)

Note on the Text

The Reverend John Gillespie Magee was born in 1884 in America and served as a missionary in Nanking, China, for twenty-eight years. Here he met Faith Backhouse, who was also a missionary, and they married and had four children. Their firstborn, a son, was christened John Gillespie

Magee, and usually Jnr is added to his title in order to differentiate him from his father.

Whenever there is any risk of ambiguity in this book, the father will be referred to as Reverend John.

Chapter 1

The Fertile Fields of Lincolnshire

It is said by wistful men who work the flat and fertile fields of Lincoln-shire that the snowflakes that hurtle horizontally across the ploughed winter furrows began their storm-swept and relentless journey on the Russian steppes.

The seemingly flat and low land of Lincolnshire forms part of the easterly seaboard of the island of England but provides no shelter from the easterly winds and thrashing sea along its coastline. Over centuries its landmass has even been extended in parts by the deposits of its lashing tides and the vagaries of swirling sand storms. In summer other winds prevail from the south-west, but further inland, where they whip up the fertile loam in blinding swirls that terminate their abrasive journey stacked up beneath the hedges that divide the land into fields and line every lane and byway.

It is those same hedges that in winter deflect the flight of the driving snow by lifting it as it approaches, dropping it in drifts that fill the very spaces they are intended to help protect – the roadways. So bad is it, so inconvenient and disruptive to travel, that false hedges, fences of wire wrapped around wooden stakes, are set in early winter, many yards back from the roadside boundaries to deceive the snow, so that it falls short of the road and piles up around the fence and on the ploughed furrows instead.[1]

Where the fence is placed is a critical distance, worked out precisely by men who for years have studied flight: the flight of snowflakes, the flight of birds and the flight of aeroplanes. These are the weathered men who work the roadside verges. They know the wind and the complex forms of drifts in sand or snow caused by a current moving against a fixed obstacle.

This land is so flat and wide that in the far distance the horizon seems to support and contain the soaring skyscapes that stretch endlessly above it. Ever since man has yearned for powered flight it has been the easiest and most obvious place to study high soaring birds but also to lay down runways and build airfields for the men who also fly. Access to that un-ending blue seems as easy as it could be and from this still and inoffensive soil pilots have flown to delirious ecstasy. Others have sojourned in its security, leaving only to attack invaders to this island and defend it against a distant enemy hell-bent on its destruction.

In the cold war, the war of nerves, it was here that secret missiles silently rose and pointed east. Motionless they waited, poised, until some hidden command sent them silently on their way. There was no discernible programme to this ritual, but everyone who knew of it was unsettled by its foreboding and unlikely presence.

This network of lanes and byways carries a patchwork of the scars of relentless planning for battles and wars that go back hundreds of years. The defence of a nation.

Central to this web of military initiative lies England's academy for training men to fly for war: Cranwell. Here some of the greatest aero-nautical inventors and aviators have tested their ideals and principles, their courage, their fear and their fantasy. For many it was the realization of a dream for which they are for ever remembered and celebrated. Even today those who aspire to fly from any walk of life come here to 'win their wings'. They come to gain the freedom to fly.

Ernest Aubrey Griffin was such a recruit. Born on 19 March 1922 at Banbury in Oxfordshire and educated at St Andrews School, Headington, and the Oxford School of Technology, he was keen to join the RAF. By June 1941 he was irritated that he had not received his call-up papers like most of his friends and so travelled to Ruislip to quicken the process of recruitment. Consequently in August he was drafted to Magdalene Coll-ege, Cambridge, to join a special course for cadets and from there he was quickly posted to RAF Peterborough.

In September 1941 he arrived at Cranwell to join Course 32, a cohort of twenty-eight carefully selected young men determined to win their free-dom to fly. The planned routines and practices for him were no different from those for the other recruits and were designed to lead progressively to the ultimate freedom, thrill and responsibility of solo flight. By Dec-ember this dedicated trainee was only weeks away from graduating and was looking forward to a posting with a multi-engine Operational Training Unit.

On 11 December 1941, the vast skyscape over Lincolnshire was filled with broken cloud. As usual the driving wind from the south-west hurried the higher billowing masses of grey and white clouds, while gaps appeared fleetingly to reveal a brighter blue in the heavens beyond. At times there was a mist of chilled rain on the wind, but this did nothing to deter those who needed to enhance their flying skills. All through the morning aircraft of various shapes and sizes roared through the sky at differing speeds and heights. Their twists and turns, drones and roars, interrupted the tranquillity of this peaceful agricultural landscape.

It was early morning on 11 December when LAC Griffin, No. 1314735, took off in his Airspeed Oxford II, T1052 trainer, on yet another routine circuit to build up his hours of flying experience. Following a standard take-off, he followed a well-rehearsed flight path, climbing to almost 500 feet just below the cloud level. The aircraft almost knew its own direction, so frequently had it followed the same routines with numerous aspiring young pilots. It was a comforting realization for this young pilot that he was secure in his handling of the aircraft through these basic routines and he settled into his cockpit seat to make the most of and enjoy the experience.

Suddenly from somewhere behind him there was a deafening roar and resounding crash and he was spinning uncontrollably earthwards. He struggled with the controls but nothing responded, and, with little or no training in emergency escape from a disintegrating aircraft, he was propelled towards the ground by the roaring engines at a terrifying speed. Impact with the ground killed him instantly. In a split second a simple routine manoeuvre had become a disaster.

This unfortunate and untimely event killed a young man in the prime of his life. But sadly this disaster had even greater repercussions that could never have been anticipated. This accident was destined to leave an indelible mark on the records of the history of flight and mark this day, time and place in history for posterity.

This disaster, caused by the collision of two aircraft, had not only taken the life of one trainee pilot but had cut short the life and career of another brilliant young man.

This book now traces and documents the life of the second young pilot in this tragedy. His name was John Gillespie Magee.

Chapter 2

Faith Backhouse

In December 1919 a small pioneering group of young men and women set sail from England to work as missionaries in China.

Their arrival was awaited with eager anticipation by the established international missionary group, who during the preceding years had slowly built up a mutually trusting relationship with the local community in and around Shanghai.

The new arrivals not only strengthened the community of missionaries but changed the social mix while increasing its potential of proclaiming Christian beliefs and values to an even wider audience.

One of the established missionaries was an American, named Billy Roberts, and he remembered the day of that arrival since he was particularly drawn to a woman in the group, the composed and attractive Faith Backhouse. It was not long before both he and his other companions were fascinated to learn how and why Faith had come to join them.

Faith, who was 28, was happy to receive this attention and to explain how she believed that her whole life and education back at home in England had been in preparation for her coming to Shanghai. 'I believe that it is God's will that I have been chosen to be here with you all, and my life until now has been a preparation to give me the strength and faith to make the most of this opportunity.'

Born on 1 October 1891, Faith Emmeline was the first of four children to be born to Mary Anne Emmeline Backhouse, née Walford, who had married the Reverend Edward Bell Backhouse on 17 April 1890 in England in the village church of Dallinghoo in Suffolk, England. Faith and her brother and sisters had been educated at home in the rectory schoolroom. Her father was acknowledged and respected in the surrounding communities for his missionary vision and ideals, and consequently his children were brought up understanding and practising Christian beliefs and values, which they shared with the constant stream of visitors to the family home.

So her commitment to missionary ideals had gradually developed over the years and been well rehearsed during her time in Suffolk. With the examples set by both her parents, she had practised Christian values in her daily support of parishioners in the nearby rural communities.

On 4 May 1889, her father, Edward Bell Backhouse, had been appointed as rector to the small rural parish of Helmingham, which lies midway between the towns of Ipswich and Stowmarket in Suffolk. She was understandably proud of his achievement of becoming a leader in this community, an achievement she described as all the more remarkable because he had been orphaned at the age of 10 and in 1867 had been sent to sea.

With virtually no education to inform his experiences, he spent the next twelve years working his passage around the world under steam and sail with the P&O Company. Faith believed that his calling to serve God and share his beliefs with others had come through his experiences while travelling the world, which had given him a tremendous personal commitment and determination. Consequently on 28 December 1882 he had handed in his notice to the shipping company and, in spite of his lack of a formal education, he took up the demanding training for Holy Orders. This took seven years, and his ordination was the culmination of an amazing personal achievement.

Faith's new-found friends gathered around her with fascination as her story unfolded, but one man was drawn to listen and watch perhaps more attentively than others in the group. He had noticed and admired her softly spoken but precise explanations and simultaneously found himself attracted to her beauty and composure. He was John Magee.

At first Faith was unaware of his attention, but it soon became obvious to her that his interests were not focused only on her family history; whenever the opportunity arose, he would take her to one side and ask her to tell him more about herself, her beliefs and ideals.

For her part, Faith wanted to know how John came to be a minister to the Episcopalian mission in Nanking and Chairman of the Nanking Committee of the International Red Cross, and was equally enthusiastic that he was delighted to share with her details of his family history.

He recounted how he was descended from Irish immigrants who in 1788 had left Coleraine or nearby Limavady, in what is now known as County Londonderry, to find the American dream. John told her how he could trace his ancestors back to a Robert Magee, born in 1737, and his wife Jane Jack, born in 1740. Together they sailed from Londonderry with their seven children to Pittsburgh and established the Magee family in America.[2] John was able to describe how from very small beginnings Robert and his family thrived, and how, as the Pittsburgh community grew in size, so their fortunes increased. Robert became a popular merchant, and, as a prominent Jeffersonian leader, he became Assistant Burgess (1802) and Chief Clerk of the market (1803). By 1805 Robert was a 'Vestryman of Trinity' and was instrumental in the establishment of the Protestant Episcopalian Church in Pittsburgh. His descendants were destined to make their mark not only as philanthropists, industrialists and politicians but also as ministers.

John was born into this widely spread, thriving and successful Pittsburgh family in October 1884. 'That', said John, 'is the origin of my faith, to my working here with the Mission in Nanking and now the good Lord has blessed me by having you to share it all with.' His clarity of thought about his missionary principles was close to Faith's ideals, and their shared beliefs and intentions drew them ever closer.

Billy Roberts, meanwhile, watched with delight as his close friend and confidant found love and companionship with Faith. He was therefore not in the least surprised when the couple announced their intention to marry. The ceremony took place in Kuling on 19 July 1921, just sixteen months after Faith had left England.

> The Pittsburgh Press, Society Section, Sunday August 28th 1921
> Cards have been received in Pittsburgh announcing the marriage
> of Miss Faith Emmeline Backhouse, daughter of the Revd and
> Mrs Edward B. Backhouse of Northwood, Middlesex, England, to
> the Revd John Gillespie Magee of Pittsburgh, which took place in
> the Church of the Ascension, Kuling, China, July 19. After Sept.
> 15th they will be at home at Nanking, China.

Eleven months later, on 12 June 1922, the *North China Daily News* announced:

> On 9th June 1922, at the Victoria Nursing Home, Shanghai, to the
> Revd and Mrs John Magee, a son.

John Gillespie Magee Jnr had been born.

As the minister at an Episcopal mission in Nanking in China, John

Magee, together with his wife Faith, faced many difficulties bringing up a family miles from their natural homelands in England and America.

Both had strong family bonds and naturally wanted their children not only to grow up as a family together but also to meet and know their grandparents, aunts and uncles living in their home countries.

When their firstborn son John was born in June 1922 in Shanghai, China, there were already growing tensions between the Chinese and Japanese nations. This made the missionary work supporting the local population in Shanghai all the more important, and the Revd John and his wife Faith were diligent in their missionary roles.

Just over three years after the birth of their first son, a second son, David Backhouse Magee, was born on 6 July 1925.

Faith was anxious to share her joy and pride in her new young family with her parents back in England, and in October of that year took them to England. The Backhouse family was delighted to meet the two new grandsons and the family bonding that Faith valued so highly began.

On her return to Shanghai, Faith found that there was an even greater need for her help and support in the local community and at the same time her two young boys presented their own demands. Not surprisingly it was decided that she needed to plan a longer respite from all these pressures and in June of the following year, 1926, she took the children to America, where they were introduced to their paternal family.

On her return to Shanghai in the late autumn of 1926 Faith was fearful for the well-being and safety of her family, and in April 1927 they moved to Maebashi in Japan.

Here the family was more settled, and on 19 August 1928 Christopher Walford Magee was born. Faith was able to spend some of her time helping her husband, and the eldest two children began their mixed-nationality nursery and kindergarten education.

But the local tensions and demands on both the Revd John and Faith made bringing up a family of three young boys very difficult. By 1930, with John now 8 years old, decisions had to be made about his future education and the rest of the family. Consequently in November 1931, John, David and Christopher sailed with their mother from Shanghai, arriving in Dover, England, in good time for Christmas. The young John Magee never returned to China, and, with Faith's parents as his guardians, he began his education in England. John's youngest brother, Frederic Hugh Magee, was born on 23 August 1933.

Chapter 3

Education: St Clare and Rugby Schools

John Magee began his education in England in January 1932 at St Clare Preparatory School for Boys at Walmer in Kent. The school was chosen for its qualities of teaching and learning but also because of its proximity to the Backhouse family home 'Foxburrow' at Kingsdown.[3]

The large house had once been the home of Lord Conyers and was first opened as a school by Alexander Murray in 1926. It was particularly popular with parents who wanted the best education for their children to prepare them for public schools. By the time John arrived at the school it was under the headship of James Vincent Hitchcock, who lived in one wing of the large house while up to twenty-five boys were educated and accommodated in the remainder.

Phyllis Carter was employed as the matron at the school and recalled how Mr Hitchcock, 'realizing the darkening cloud over Europe . . . evacuated St Clare in September 1938 to Glastonbury in Somerset'.

While St Clare served John's immediate schooling needs, as he approached his 10th birthday it was decided that he should continue his education at Rugby School. Recalling the later years at St Clare and the first years at Rugby, Faith's sister June remembered: 'My father Edward Backhouse must have been responsible for John, as his parents seemed to be always in China or the US. I think the school reports were sent to him and he dealt with the schools.' Whatever the arrangement the choice could not have been better, and John eagerly settled into his new life at Rugby. He quickly came under the influence of the headmaster, Hugh Lyon, who, as part of his duties, supervised one of the houses in which different groups of boys lived. His house was School House. Rugby had traditions going back to its greatest headmaster, Thomas Arnold, and had developed on principles of freedom encompassed with exacting discipline and responsibility.

In Hugh Lyon John found a paternal discipline and love enhanced by Hugh's professional insight and understanding of the English language and particularly poetry.

Under this leadership John's academic achievements blossomed, but with it came an intolerance of routines, and he was frequently trying to push back the boundaries. 'What he has to learn', a school report explains, 'is restraint both in matter and manner, and more patience in criticism.' Hugh Lyon wrote of him: 'He was impatient of drudgery and detail but he had a shrewd eye for what mattered in life and in work.'

But headmasters of the calibre of Hugh had an instinctive understanding of the boys in their care. Hugh sensed and even anticipated John's outstanding talent and adventurous spirit which was frequently exasperated by constraint. One particular incident illustrates this very well.

As he waited with others in his year in the queue for lunch, John had been handed a note by a senior boy. He casually opened it and, surveying the handwritten note, quickly realized that this summons was an announcement of what he had been dreading.

It was a typically depressing grey autumn afternoon as John reluctantly made his way to his appointment. He had known from the outset that it would only be a matter of time before he would be summoned to account for himself, and he now waited for his punishment with a sense of imminent nausea. He knew that yet again he had overstepped the boundaries in his late-night excursion, breaking all school rules. He had bragged about doing it for nearly a week. Doing it was one thing but getting caught or found out was another. Now called before the Master, Hugh Lyon, to account for himself was not just terrifying but sickening. He hated himself.

He climbed the echoing stone staircase to the Master's study door and tapped carefully to announce his arrival. There was no reply. He coughed, once, twice, as if this might signal his presence and looked around him in the gloomy corridor, wondering what to do next. It was not the first time he had been summoned to appear before the Master; he knew the routines and punishments that were likely to follow, probably a flogging.

'Magee.' The Master's voice rattled the suspense as he appeared from the staircase. 'Come in and stand there,' he said, opening the office door and pointing to a place in front of a large desk covered with piles of books and documents.

The muscles in John's buttock tightened as he entered the familiar surroundings, his mouth was dry and he was trembling with fear.

'Last night,' the Master began, 'you went beyond the bounds of all reason and, as the one and only person in this school who has complete authority to punish you for your thoughtless behaviour . . .'

The words droned on and on, but somehow John was not listening, and instead his mind was anticipating the flogging that was certain to begin in moments. He wished he could get it over.

He tried to stop the Master's intonation, which seemed to be addressed to the wall behind him, by interrupting.

'I'm sorry Sir,' he began, but it made no difference. The Master's words continued to describe previous misdemeanours as if he was not there. He tried again.

'I'm sorry Sir,' he repeated, seemingly again without effect. He sighed in desperation. At that second the Master stopped and looked straight at him and with a furrowed brow announced:

'Magee, I've tried to understand your outbursts of thoughtless behaviour, I've listened to your stream of excuses and explanations and I have reached the end of accommodating your stupidity.'

He paused and demanded: 'Look at me, John. I need to find a way to help you, to help you to behave responsibly and appropriately to our school, to your year and house, and to me acting for you "in loco parentis". Once again you have let us all down.'

'But Sir,' began John.

'No John,' the Master interrupted. 'No more of your lucid explanations. I've heard it all. There can be no more excuses. I've one last opportunity in mind to make you come to your senses.'

With that he moved to the door and ordered John to follow him, adding that he should speak to no one along the way.

The Master set off briskly down the stone steps and into the quad-rangle below. Boys they met stepped aside courteously for the Master but sniggered and gestured at John, who followed close behind. He felt as if something terrible was about to happen and kept his eyes down, following the Master's footsteps.

On the far side of the quadrangle they came to a studded oak door set back in the stonework. Stopping, the Master pulled a bunch of keys from beneath his flowing black gown and unlocked the bolted door.

'After you,' he gestured to John, who was relieved to go anywhere that escaped the leering gestures of other boys.

'Go to the top of the steps,' came the order, and, as he started to ascend, he heard the door close and lock click behind him and footsteps then follow him.

In the half-light he could just make out the steep stone spiral stairs curling upwards. The air was chill and dank, and as he reached the top it opened into a small room with a boarded wooden floor. There was little daylight that penetrated the two begrimed oriole windows, and the room echoed with his footsteps.

'Now sit on that chair,' came the order.

Fearful of what was now going to happen, John obeyed and perched motionless on a worn wooden seat that was more like a pew than a chair. The Master sat on the only other piece of furniture in the room, a heavily carved blackened oak chest, which was pushed up close to the wall under one of the two windows.

'I've brought you here for a reason. It's my final desperate attempt to bring you to your senses. This room is kept locked and I have the only key, which was given to me by my predecessor. I come here as he did to think and to reflect on what has been and what might be and what must be. To help you I want to appeal to a side of you, a part of you, that has not yet matured and grown as it should. You know from all the writings of the great authors I have shared with you in our study, of the very best literature, that outstanding writers and poets of the past searched in their hearts and reflected on life in order better to understand their real purposes and intentions. You need to learn to begin to do this now.'

'I don't generally bring boys here, but I have decided to make an exception and bring you here to this, my private space, and share it with you. Why? Because a past pupil of this school, whose writing I know you have come to admire and love and wish to emulate, came to this room frequently to contemplate. Yes, Rupert Brooke. Look there.'

He pointed to below the window.

'In the stone he even scratched that inscription. Perhaps you recognize it as the opening line of that poem we spent so long discussing in class.'

Without looking at either the inscription or John, in the fading light he recited the line that he and John both knew by heart.

'Here in the dark, O heart, Alone with the enduring Earth and Night.'

They both sat and, reflecting in the still silence for several minutes, he then concluded:

'You need to acquire the kind of deeper feeling and understanding which that poem explores to sustain and guide you in the difficult days and years ahead. Reflect on what you really want to do with your life, what is really important to you. Do I make myself clear?'

As John was about to reply, the Master raised his hand in a gesture of silence. 'No, I think we understand each other. I will leave the keys with you, and, when you have taken as much time as you need, you will return the keys to me at my home, personally. Understood?'

He raised his eyebrows as an indication that John need not reply, because the principles were agreed between them, turned and walked slowly down the echoing steps, leaving John alone.

John sat for some time without moving and then slowly walked to the scratched words and ran his fingers across the letters. He mused for some time, he tried to look out across the courtyard, and then, fumbling in his jacket pocket, he found a pen and an odd piece of folded paper. Sitting on the floor and using the oak chest as a table he began to write.

Ideas flooded into his mind, words formed, were noted, held and discarded, and then gradually took on a shape, a poem.

> This is a monstrous night!
> It presses on my ears, my eyes
> As if to crush out of me
> That very soul which I am proud
> To call my own. I hear no sound
> Except the urgent
> Ticking of a clock, and some busy whisper
> Of the wind. Above, the stars
> Have hid their aspen-faces from
> My eager eyes; and somewhere in this
> Thick impenetrable gloom, there is
> Reality.
> Its shape, its form, its depth
> I cannot know. Incomprehensible.
> A feeling, not a thing: but this I know:
> A hand stretched out to mine. A voice
> Whispered a secret to my soul.
>
> Oh inspiration! Here I have found you!
> – You came to me for one brief,
> Ecstatic moment – and are gone.
> You showed me a glimpse of
> Something beyond. So Life
> Is not in vain! There is an End!
> The night is clearer now. The stars

> Gaze blankly down, like wistful children,
> – And it is still . . .

It was late evening by the time the words came together in their final form. More than three hours had passed on the quadrangle's tower clock when John eventually locked the door behind him and made his way in the darkness to the Master's house. He paused before the doorway and pulled the bell rope, hoping that Elinor, the Master's eldest daughter, would answer. Eventually a key turned in the door and it was opened by Barbara, the Master's second daughter, who, recognizing him, left John on the doorstep and went to find her father.

John glanced into the dimly lit hallway hoping to see Elinor. He then heard the Master's voice in the distance tell Barbara simply to take the keys and say goodnight, since it was very late and he had nothing further to say.

She skipped back to the doorway and held out her hand for the keys. Taking them, she smiled knowingly, as if reading John's thoughts, and slowly closing the door wished him goodnight.

It had been seven hours since John had been summoned to account for himself. Hugh Lyon had redirected his purpose and changed his life.

Chapter 4

Crossing the Atlantic to America

On 2 August 1939 the Cunard 'White Star' liner *Queen Mary* prepared to set sail from Southampton. The journey would follow a scheduled route via Cherbourg and, according to an extract from the log, the passage was planned to take '4 days, 15 hours and 3 minutes'.

Dermott Magill had shared a study at Rugby with John, and now the two of them were about to embark on the holiday of a lifetime, travelling to New York to go to the World Fair and then to give John the chance to re-establish relationships with the Magees and his wider family. By prior arrangement, John's father had arranged for his sister Mary Scaife to meet, accommodate and look after John and Dermott.

The journey across the Atlantic was detailed in a journal kept by Dermott, which described the other passengers as 'a really mixed lot'. 'There are the retired film star type, the budding film stars, the box camera and orange type, the portly French, one of which is stroking his beard next to me, and there are also some of which are very nice. The majority of passengers on this class are Americans.'[4]

They shared a third-class cabin – its only fault being that it had no port-hole[5] – and revelled in touring the separate parts of the ship and comparing the quality of provision of different passenger classes. Not surprisingly, the next morning, Thursday, 3 August, John was immediately searching out the unusual parts of the ship and quickly determined to climb to the crow's nest. Several of the crew laughed at his intention, saying it was 180 feet above the deck and out of bounds to passengers, which simply made John the more determined. At midday, accompanied by Dermott, they slipped into the crew's quarters, found access, and, with John leading, ascended the 110 steps of the ladder to the top. John knew no fear and Dermott followed trembling but not wanting to be thought a coward.

The view from the top was stunning; the wind speed, headwind plus the speed of the liner, was about 30 knots. John threw his arms around Dermott and was to be heard above the roar of the wind and waves shouting: 'I feel like I'm a bird discovering the sky.'

That night, at about 11.15, the vessel ran into fog, and every five minutes the siren blasted its warning to oncoming shipping. They stood on deck in the bow of the ship astonished that, in spite of the fog, 'this huge ship seemed to be racing over the water'.

As on all great liners, entertainment catered for every type of passenger, and having found seats next to three attractive girls in the cinema, they marvelled at Loretta Young and Don Ameche in *The Modern Miracle* and then, embracing the girls, they 'danced the night away' in the Garden Lounge.[6]

Saturday, 5 August, was a morning of recovery from the night before, daredevil gate-crashing of Tourist Class Only facilities, then more dancing followed by 'horse racing' in the Garden Lounge. When they met up again with the girls from the previous evening, it turned out that they were heading home to Martha's Vineyard, and addresses and contact details were exchanged.

Sunday, 6 August, brought unusual discomforts. At about 2.00 a.m. the liner was in the Gulf Stream, the air hot, damp and clammy. Dermott wrote: 'In the morning we were sweating like nips.' Beginning to adjust to the humidity, they attended mid-morning Divine Service in the Main Cabin Lounge, went to the 'Farewell Dinner' in the evening in the Garden Lounge, then, finding the girls again, danced until the band stopped at 11.00pm. 'But that didn't deter us,' Dermott recorded. 'We took them with us and crashed the Tourist Lounge, and when they stopped moved on again and danced till dawn.'

In the early morning thick fog enshrouded the Manhattan skyline but the night revellers, 'still in evening clothes', cheered and embraced when, 'just after passing a small island on the starboard side, they suddenly saw the Statue of Liberty rising out of a light silvery mist'.

Travelling up the Hudson River to Dock 90 gave both John and Dermott their first impressions of the New York skyline, 'buildings rising out of the mist towering straight up into the sky'. They finally docked at 10.00 a.m. and disembarked to be met by John's aunt Mary Scaife. She took them to the Beverley Hotel on 50th Street, where she had booked them into rooms adjoining her own on the fifteenth floor. They were swept off their feet by the style and glamour of it all, the contrasts with their tiny room at Rugby and the prospect of what was to come.

Tuesday, 8 August, brought greater contrasts. They visited the Empire State Building, chiefly because John wanted to know what it felt like to be 1,200 feet above ground level. Everything fascinated him, the speed of the elevator, how high each level was, even the number of windows. Within hours they were off again to the World Trade Fair, where, in spite of them having that morning bought lightweight shirts and trousers, they were almost overcome by the heat. Back then to New York to meet up with Aunt Mary, who had purchased tickets in advance for a show, *Streets of Paris*, then to 'La Rue' nightclub and dancing until early morning.

'Aunt Mary was determined we should do everything in New York; it all seemed too good to be true,' John later wrote in a letter to his parents. Mary had been resolute from the outset of her plan that he should experience the lifestyle they expected as a family. This was an opportunity for him to get to know his relatives and fatherland, before they forgot him and he lost contact with them altogether.

With return tickets booked on the *Mauritania* in time to be back in England for the commencement of the term at Rugby, Aunt Mary planned successive weeks of hospitality in Pittsburgh. John and Dermott, however, were missing the comforts and assurances of their dancing partners, whom they had left with tearful farewells at New York Grand Central train station. The prospect of moving to Pittsburgh and finding new friends simply offered another round of romantic and flirtatious relationships. John wrote:

> Always there will be loves that drift, as ours
> Beautiful faces, toughened by fresher winds
> Change suddenly – and soon are blown away
> Passion forgets her few, ecstatic hours
> Soon after, in new hearts, and other minds
> And finds enchantment for another day.

It was almost 140 years since the Magees had travelled from Ireland and established their family roots in Pittsburgh as early settlers. Now Aunt Mary wanted her nephew to meet his relations and understand the generations of accomplishment over which the family now presided. The Scaifes owned the largest coal company in the world and were typical of the larger family's many successes in other industries. Because of the family's financial prosperity, Aunt Mary was able to afford to pay for

Nanking, China. John Magee Jnr is at the front left, described on the back of the photograph as 'one of the merry men'. 'Robin Hood' school play, May 1930.

Deal, 1933. John Magee (centre) with brothers Christopher (left) and David (right). *All pictures in this section are from a private collection unless credited otherwise.*

On holiday, Deal, circa 1933. Shooting practice. John Magee on left.

John Magee at St Clare, Walmer.

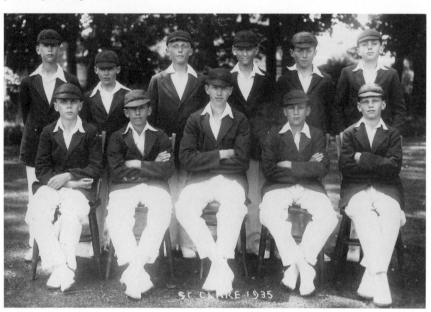

St Clare School cricket team, 1935. John Magee, back row first right.

St Clare School, Walmer, Kent (taken between 1932 and 1935). John Magee, second from right, with headmaster James Vincent Hitchcock on John's left.

Deal, England, 1936. John Magee (second from the left) with school friends.

John Magee in North Wales, 1936.

The Reverend John Gillespie Magee.

The Magee family, circa 1938.

Lake District holiday with the Lyon family, April 1937. John Magee is far right with Hugh Lyon behind and Elinor in the centre.

Lake District holiday, 1937, at the foot of Helvellyn. John Magee, far right. Dermott Magill, second from right. Hugh Lyon, far left.

Lake District holiday, 1937. John stands left of picture on Striding Edge with Elinor on the right.

Lake District holiday. Picnic on Lake Windermere. From left to right, Elinor Lyon, unknown, John, Barbara Lyon.

Hugh and Nan Lyon in the Lake District.

Elinor Lyon, WRNS.

Left to right, Elinor, Jill, Christopher and
Barbara Lyon, 1941.

Elinor (left) and Barbara Lyon.

John Magee at Rugby School, 1938.

John Magee, Mortehoe, spring 1938.

John Magee, 16 years old, with his mother, Faith, receiving the poetry prize at Rugby School, 1939.

John Magee, Avon Old Farms School, Connecticut, high school graduation portrait, 1940.

Rugby School, School House photograph, 1938. John Magee is third row, fourth from the right with Dermott Magill on his right. *Ivan Henson Collection*

Avon Old Farms School, Connecticut.

John Magee (left) with Douglas Eves on a visit to Stratford in 1939.

John Magee (left) on board the *Queen Mary* with Dermott Magill – on their way to the New York World's Fair in 1939.

John in Dermott Magill's room at Oriel, Oxford, 1941.

John to stay at the most prestigious social club – set in 40,000 acres of prime Pennsylvania countryside, the Rolling Rock Club.

The young people of Pittsburgh who were able to afford to entertain and be entertained by the extravagances of the Rolling Rock made it easy for John to forget the 'romantic liaisons' of the *Queen Mary*, and he threw himself into the general melee of being an active participant in every kind of amusement, whatever the cost.

Aunt Mary had never anticipated how rapidly John would fully explore his new-found opportunities, and when she was sent the account for payment for a stay of only two weeks, she and her close relatives were indignant at John's extravagance. Writing to his father some time later, she acknowledged that he had tried to keep up with 'a pretty fast set to whom money was nothing'. It is not surprising that, with little or no parental guidance to hand, he had taken everything on offer, without question!

As his relatives admonished him for his thoughtless behaviour, they seem to have ignored their own responsibilities to him. Once faced with the reality, he withdrew from the social scene and became quite depressed and homesick, needing his true friends around him. He longed for the security of the Lyons family, of Rugby, but particularly of Elinor.

The day was fast approaching for the return journey on the *Mauritania*. For John it could not come quickly enough, so that he could escape his family's disapproval of his behaviour. Then, on 1 September 1939, Germany declared war. The consequences were to have an immediate impact on John's future.

John responded to this act of belligerence with a mixture of despair and outrage. He wanted to embrace and protect his beloved England and was intolerant of relatives who suggested that it was a war that had nothing to do with him because he was an American citizen.

John had other ideas. He felt isolated from his natural family, his mother, brothers and grandparents, and more especially from his adopted family at Rugby. The decisive moment came when he was refused a passport by the American State Department. In a letter to Douglas Eves, who had been a close friend at Rugby School, John wrote:

> I am stranded here in America so far from where I need to be.
> I have been under a sort of emotional stress ever since the war
> began, and I realised I was in a spot, as being unable to get back
> home . . . I am feeling terribly homesick . . . I shall never be really
> happy over here. Don't you believe a man should live by his

convictions? I am convinced my place is in England, and if ever I see the opportunity, I'm coming.[7]

While that might have been his optimistic hope, there was little or no chance of it being realized. Aunt Mary, acting in loco parentis, now had a problem: what to do with John? He was uncomfortable in the presence of his American aunts and uncles and was argumentative. He disagreed with their proposal that he should finish his schooling in America: 'There can be no school here to compare with Rugby and since I cannot return I'll get a job.'[8]

In spite of not having any work experience, he thought he might become a tutor; an unrealistic dream, his relatives told him, and he resigned himself to schooling. The family decided he should attend Avon Old Farms School and achieve high-enough qualifications to be accepted in the family tradition at Yale University.

Avon Old Farms School was an all boys' school and not chosen at random. Its low brick buildings surrounded by trees and playing fields were set just 120 miles north of New York in a rural environment close to Hartland. It was a clever choice, since it outwardly reflected the romantic style of English architecture with which John was familiar at Rugby. Aunt Mary completed the registration form on 4 October 1939 and made the first down payment of school fees.

Once settled in, John was at least within the regulated framework of a school, and his daily physical needs were catered for in a manner to which he was accustomed. His mental turmoil continued, however, and he needed parental leadership, particularly from his father, who was still fully engaged in his missionary work in Nanking. His commitment to helping safeguard Chinese families in the city was total – and during the storming of Nanking in December 1937 and in the months that followed, regardless of his own safety, he was an instrumental figure in saving 250,000 citizens within the safety zone set up in the city. Every moment of every day he worked to provide help and support to the beleaguered people whom he loved throughout one of the world's greatest atrocities.[9] Not surprisingly, with his wife and children safe in Kent, missionary John Magee had had little time to concern himself about John, his eldest son. With his father's principles determining that he stay in China, John felt cut off from his father and the family isolated in America. In a long letter to his father, in August 1940, John concluded 'you have given me the impression that you no longer have faith in me'.[10]

School, meanwhile, provided intellectual challenges, and it was not long before John was once again caught up in his discoveries of classical literature. In addition, he sought out teachers who would encourage him, listen to his often unresolved ideas and help him to shape his ideals. One such person was Max Stein, who was in charge of the school's print shop and helped John to bring together the best of the many poems he had written and publish them in a book. Cost determined that only a small quantity could be printed, perhaps twenty, and an attempt in March 1940 to have more printed by a publisher in New York, Charles Scribner, was not successful.

The book had been meticulously prepared under Stein's supervision, and it was under his guidance that John wrote the light-hearted foreword suggesting that, while the poems might be 'permitted by the Muses to give some pleasure', they should be read 'not too critically'.

The selection includes poems and fragments of poems written at different times over the previous four years. John was not yet 18 years old. Some are carefully scripted and reflect the influences of acknowledged poets such as Rupert Brooke. Others are clearly exercises exploring the poetic muse, under the direction of highly skilled teaching at Rugby. More importantly, his writing reveals a love of, and passion for, the poetic form of expression. These poems are the foundation on which later writings were created.

As term progressed, John became even more determined to do things his own way and get back to England as quickly as possible. But, under pressure from his uncle and advice from the Dean of Avon, Richard Sears, applications were made for scholarships to both Yale and Harvard. By early summer both had responded to 'this first class candidate' by offering him a place for the next academic year.[11] It was simply a matter of choosing which university, but John continued to argue for his return to England, unimpressed by the scholarship offers.

But Uncle Jim, James Magee, had other ideas. In his offices at 612 Magee Building, New York, he was upset and indignant that John had turned down an invitation to visit at Easter and reprimanded him. 'You are very English, which is quite to be expected. If you will pardon my saying so, tactlessness is characteristic of English people. There is no more complacent, self-satisfied race on earth than the British! . . . Certainly there is no immediate prospect of you going back to England. I think it is settled. . .'[12]

Settled it was. Clearly Uncle Jim had been in regular contact with John's

father and mother in taking a firm line with John, but had probably also
told them that John needed his close family around him. From different
parts of the world they arrived almost simultaneously in New York in
time for their son's 18th birthday on 9 June – three days after he had
graduated from Avon Old Farms School. Academic success at Avon,
Harvard or Yale seemed inconsequential, and the arrival of his close
family did not seem to ease the anguish. In a letter to his friend Geoffrey he
described his frustration: 'My own natural enthusiasm for things is being
slowly smothered . . . at times I think I am going mad with yearning, the
vain and insistent groping to be back in the past, when the wind blew in
my face from the Channel, and all was ecstasy. They won't let me back
to England . . . the poetry is dying in me. . . . I am like a fish out of water.'

Desperation drove him even further and he wrote directly to the Secretary
of War for the Canadian Government.

> August 16th 1940 [John Magee is 18]
> His Excellency the Secretary of War
> Canadian National Government, Ottawa.
> Excellency.
>
> Not knowing to whom I should write in order to secure the
> information I need, I have presumed to trespass on your time, which
> I am sure is not over bountiful at this time, in the hope that, should
> you not have time to read this missive yourself, you will yet be so
> kind as to see that it reaches the appropriate department of the
> Canadian War Office.
>
> I am half English (my father being American) and indeed count
> myself English in everything but actual birth, having lived the best
> part of my life in England including the last ten years. I was
> educated at St Clare, and subsequently at Rugby School, where I
> spent four years.
>
> During a sort of celebratory trip to this country on being admitted
> to Oxford University last summer, I found myself to be here when
> war broke out. I was at once deprived of my passport, and refused
> permission to return home by the State Department in Washington.
> After several attempts to find a job I was admitted at half fees to

Avon Old Farm (School) in Connecticut as a post graduate and graduated with distinction this June.

My chances of getting home look a deal more dismal than they did last Autumn. I am desperately anxious to do something to help England just now. It does not seem to me to be a question of whether one more man will make a difference as it does to be a moral issue, as to whether I can sit pretty over here while my family and friends are suffering. The only thing I could possibly do, it appears, would be to join the Canadian Air Force in order to hit back at the Teutonic Juggernaut and it is in the hope of being accepted for some sort of service that I am writing this letter.[13]

John's birthday celebration on 9 June meant that the Reverend John[14] at last had all his family together in one place. He was determined to make the most of the opportunity so that everyone could get to know each other again. John had misgivings. He believed he had changed and become very independent. 'I have had to take the reins of my own life in hand.'

In truth, John was quickly taken up in family affairs and excited at the prospect of planning a holiday on an island known as Martha's Vineyard, located south of Cape Cod and known as being an affluent summer colony. The family arranged to take a cottage near the small town of Oak Bluffs on the north-east of the island, and John was in his element surrounded by, and leading, his brothers in a series of wild excursions and games.

The need to access the best of everything was facilitated by the purchase of a second-hand open-top Packard car, duly christened Mephistopheles. John drove it with a reckless abandon for the family, with the family, and also as a means of contacting and impressing others of his age, girls and boys who were experiencing the freedoms summer holidays by the sea could offer.

John taking girls for a spin in Mephistopheles caused his anxious father considerable concern. Sometimes, without explanation, John left in the morning and did not return until late evening. A girl named Phyllie was one of his companions on these excursions down narrow coastal tracks at high speed, both of them shouting to be heard over the incessant roar of the troubled engine and the gusting wind.

Peace and quiet came as a necessary contrast among isolated sand dunes; as they lay back in the sand, the heat of the sun seemed less than the heat from the sun-drenched dunes. It was here that 'Phyll and I watched the high clouds drifting in cream wisps against an azure blue; lesser formations scudded in below and seemed quickly dispersed. I have the sensation of inverted vertigo,' he confided in her, 'seeming almost to float upwards.'[15]

Turning his left hand over in hers, she pointed to his index finger. 'Tell me about that mark,' she begged. 'It's a secret,' he teased. 'I don't tell anyone about that unless they are special, so I might tell you one day.' She giggled and held his hand tightly, floating too. There were none of the familiar indicators of time and space. He turned to her. 'Can you feel the azure envelop you – it spreads sideways and upwards as if for ever. I just feel that oneness with the creator of it all; just think', he smiled, 'all this we know together today will go on for ever.' She smiled back, released his hand and drew him towards her. 'You're so sure aren't you; you say things I've felt but never found words for.' Their lips met as they sank back into the sand.

As a playground the long undulating coastline was ideal, but it also provided time and place for another fascination, whether he was with Phyllie or other friends. He would watch the sea birds in focused silence and then later at night describe the experience to his family, or anyone who would listen.

Today, again I watched the seabirds hovering high up, sea eagles, their dive bombing the sea is the most fearful attack from the sky I have ever seen. They are so well designed for attack. When they see prey they dive vertically in such a menacing and efficient way and when they hit the water it is unbelievable. Twice I have been near enough to even hear the contact as well as see it.

The fish have no chance and as they are hauled out of the water by its talons it turns the fish so the head is pointing forwards; it is aerodynamics.

They are totally efficiently designed to even strike fear – but it isn't necessary, the fish are totally unaware of their imminent death. It comes in a moment and the efficiency of the flight attack is so awe inspiring and admirable that there is little thought for the culling of the fish.

Such vivid description brought admiration, on the one hand, and unease as well, particularly when John concluded one such account: 'They are fearsome predators designed for sea patrol and efficiency of attack. Oh, how I would love to fly like the eagle!'

Phyllie just giggled and reminded him how she had first met him. She was a pupil at Miss Porter's Academy for girls, just 4 miles from Avon, which was exclusively for boys. The two schools had regularly joined together for social events. On one evening, with 100 or more boys and girls watching, John had climbed a towering tree to save a kitten that was howling with fear in the upper branches. She reminded him how they had all been terrified that he might fall, and amazed at the speed and agility of the climb and the safe return of the kitten to ground level.

'You were wonderful – so brave,' she said.

'It was nothing,' he modestly replied. 'I would do anything to protect or save an animal – I mean it – I would do it for anyone, anything and especially you!'

Days on the beach, dances and parties – Phyllie joined John and friends on a continuous round of entertainment and fun. When he was criticized for his wild and sometimes irresponsible behaviour, his retort, particularly to his parents, was blunt and hurtful: 'My generation does not expect to live long, and we want to enjoy ourselves while we may.'

But there were also other important ideas occupying his mind. As he studied the sea eagles, it was clear that he was developing a closely observed understanding of the way of their manœuvring, the use of rising air currents, the height of the seemingly lazy hovering and coasting and the steep dive, wings half closed, claws stretched forward and the awesome crashing of entry into the sea, emerging within seconds victorious with a fish.

Phyllie marvelled at his enthusiasm and knowledge.

'Do you know everything about everything?' she questioned.

'Not quite,' he responded, kissing her on the cheek, and teasing her: 'just wait, one day I will be as good as *Pandion haliaetus*, that's its proper Latin name you know!' They laughed.

Meanwhile, the news of the horrors of the Battle of Britain swept across the Atlantic. America watched as British and Commonwealth pilots displayed heroism and self-sacrifice to hold back Hitler's continuous and devastating attack from the air.

By early September a decision about John's future was pressing in on John – and his parents. He pleaded with them to let him defer the places he had been offered at Yale and Harvard. 'I just can't go to Yale. I never felt so deeply about anything before. I have got to get into this and join the Royal Canadian Air Force.'

With his parents' consent, he went to Yale to meet the President, Charles Seymour, an old friend of his father, to explain his reasoning. 'Charlie' later recounted their meeting to John's father. Having himself been educated in England and having sent his son to England for schooling, he appreciated that John had already made up his mind and did little to dissuade him.

So, with friends, family and academics all giving their different advice, John spent the last few days of September in a turmoil of anticipation and emotional farewells.

'I feel he is too young to go to war,' wrote his father. 'My wife and I feel we should not oppose him in this desire as it might embitter him, but God only knows when the thing will be over or when he will return, if ever.'[16]

Chapter 5

Learning to Fly

The German Luftwaffe continued its bombardment of England with terrifying regularity. News from Europe was agonizing, and it was reported that the air attacks were penetrating deeper into England, with huge air raids on strategic cities and ports. John was only too aware of this and also realized that many of his Rugby friends were 'taking the King's shilling'. Indeed, some had already been killed.

In October 1940, John officially enlisted in the Royal Canadian Air Force in Montreal. Details of his movements during the last months of 1940 are dependent almost entirely on letters to his parents and to staff at Avon Old Farms School and at Rugby. The explanations of the tedious routines he had to fulfil are written with verve and optimism, and extracts from them describe his frustrations, delights and determination.

4 October 1940
Terrible fortune has befallen me. Having gone to Ottawa and had an interview even with Air Marshall Breadner himself, I came back to Montreal and put in my application for the Air Force. I got my interview and medical right away (yesterday) but was found to be 16 pounds underweight. So they told me to go away and put on some weight and come back in two weeks. Since then I have been eating myself sick at every meal, drinking milk, stout etc., ad infin., given up smoking and all forms of exercise and sleeping 10 or 11 hours at night. Have gained half a pound. I only have to gain 4 to 6 pounds for them to accept me. (They will overlook 10 pounds underweight but not 16 pounds.) What on earth am I going to do? I've simply got to get in, I'll die of chagrin if I don't. If determination will get me in, I'm in. This extra two weeks sitting around is rather unfortunate as it will be quite a drag on finances . . . I can't tell you

how miserable I am. Give me some hints about getting fat![17]

19 October 1940
I have some good news for you – I passed my medical test with
flying colours, having gone from 137 to 152 pounds in 6 days. I am
actually overweight the second time! So now I am A. C./2 Magee,
His Majesty's Royal Canadian Air Force. I really can't believe it, it's
all happening so quickly – if it's true! . . . I am expecting any day
now to be sent to my initial training school in Brandon, Manitoba,
45 hours west by train.

24 October 1940
No. 1 – Manning Depot, Toronto, Canada
Since I last wrote you I have been moved to Toronto. I arrived here
on Friday morning with a snorting cold, and feeling very miserable
after sitting up all night on the train. The first thing we were told on
arriving was that we were automatically C. B. for 72 hours. So since
then I didn't even see the sky, until this morning, when we were
allowed out on the grounds.

   The barracks here are situated on the grounds on an obsolete
exposition and we are living in the actual exposition buildings, which
is all very well except for the fact it is so terribly overcrowded. The
Air Force is terribly congested and disorganized just now, and it's a
matter of luck as to whether we spend a week or month here. This
is simply what is known as a Manning Pool where we are issued
with uniforms, inoculated, etc.

   I sleep in a large hall with about 1,500 other men in two-layer
berths, but they are not too bad, really. The food is not designed
for the most sensitive palates, as you can imagine, but that is just
one of the Ardua to be undergone before the Astra comes in sight . . .

   I have just learnt that it will be impossible for me to get back to
the States, even for Christmas, as I would be interned as a
belligerent, so it looks as if we may not see each other till the war
is over. Rather a horrible thought, but – 'C'est la guerre!'

The next development in his training was a move to Trenton, Ontario,
which was a holding station, pending a vacancy at an Initial Training
School. From there he wrote of more frustrations.

29 October 1940

I have been drafted from Toronto to this place, which is the biggest
RAF Aerodrome in Canada. I am here on 'Security Guard', that is
sentry duty until there is a place for me at I.T.S. [Initial Training
School]. None of us were told anything about this long and tedious
ordeal when we joined up, and even at Manning Pool they told us
we would only be here about two weeks at the outside, but now we
find that we shall be lucky to be in I.T.S. by Christmas. . . . Every
man here wants with all his heart to be a pilot; . . . the only thing
we can be sure of is England by the summer. I can hardly believe it!
I only wish I had joined up long ago so that I should be there now.

I am writing this on sentry guard between 1.00 and 5.00 a.m. at
night; it's bitterly cold, I'm writing in gloves, which is why this is
so illegible. Strictly verboten and all that! I'm in a sand-bagged
machine gun post, with a Lewis gun in front of me filled with 500
rounds of incendiary ammunition. From my vantage point I can
rake the whole aerodrome, if need be. This is indeed a symbolic and
powerful position. Above me the stars, in all their brittle intensity,
seem to watch with me through the long night's vigil and I am not
alone. With all its discomforts, this is the life! The throb of an
aeroplane engine is music in my ears now. It has all the power of
Beethoven, the grandeur of Wagner, and the eagerness and intensity
of Strauss . . . I have become one of a group of men, who are all,
to the last man, resigned to death and even anxious for it – or if
not for death, at least for the chance of showing their mettle. Talk
of the war is verboten among us. We speak only of the past and the
present. The future for us does not exist. It is no good trying to talk
reason to any of us. We are living deliberately in a sort of fool's
paradise.

An aeroplane is to us not a weapon of war, but a flash of silver
slanting the skies; the hum of a deep voiced motor; a feeling of
dizziness; it is speed and ecstasy.

The poet in John was never far away, and he managed to use his skills
with the shaping of words to give insight into the principles and ideals of
those around him. Writing to Max Stein back at Avon, he requested that
he send him two copies of his book of poems, and also asked his parents
to send him a copy of his Rugby School prize-winning poem 'Brave New
World'. With time on his hands when on guard duty or checking entry

passes, he found the poetic language broke the boredom. 'Tonight I have been standing at the main gate of the aerodrome examining passes, under the magnificent and sort of baronial tutelage of the Aurora Borealis.' Jim Coyne, on guard duty with him, recalled 'Magee was a smart cookie – he always had a way with words.'

With a short break with his family for Christmas, the New Year promised the real experiences he was waiting for. On 15 January 1941 he wrote to his parents and almost as a postscript added: 'Am now "Aircraftman – First Class" and when I graduate from here on the 28th (if) will be L/A/C (Leading Aircraftman) – then a long wait before becoming either Sergeant-Pilot or Pilot Officer. But that's in the very distant future!'

And four days later, 19 January 1941:

My Maths final is tomorrow so characteristically enough I am spending the most important evening here, writing letters! I shall be posted to Elementary Flying School at the end of this week. I finally did well in my Link, ending up with 92%. 94% is the highest ever recorded. I think I shall pass my Maths –I am not afraid of my medical, which I shall have on Tuesday. My Squadron Commander is recommending me for a commission.

On 27 January 1941, with the course completed in Elementary Flying Training, John became Leading Aircraftman. On the 28th he received his Pilot Flying Log Book, and John Gillespie Magee was given his entry code J/5823 and took up his flying training at St Catharine's Flying School.

This has the reputation of being the toughest station in the whole of Canada [he wrote with pride].

We started in flying at once and after six hours[18] soloed (Feb. 3rd). I was the first in my class of 24 to solo, and beat the record for this station which was 6:50. The average is 10 to 11 hours. My instructor was most encouraging. Said I was the most exceptional pupil he had ever had, and he thought I would be a valuable man in the service, etc. Result, J.G.M, cheers up a bit. (The instructors are Air Force trained civilians.)

At last the dream was beginning to turn into reality, and the self-belief, flair and absence of any fear of flying gave him huge confidence. But that confidence would be best described as exuberance and sometimes led to inexplicable and often irresponsible actions.

On 5 February John's log book shows another training flight with his principal flying instructor, Flying Officer Alexander Paterson. This is then followed by two more solo flights, but against the first of these two entries there is an exclamation mark. A possible explanation of this seemingly insignificant detail comes from two sources, the first from another flying instructor at St Catharine's named Alan Stinton.[19]

There was another side to this young man which I hesitate to mention. Despite his brilliant mind, educated at Rugby in England, a scholarship to Yale in U.S.A. and his above average ability as a pilot, he was very temperamental, wanted to do his own thing and was very impatient with the slowness of learning to fly. He wanted to get on with it, get to the next phase and get into action overseas so that he could contribute to the cause of freedom.

One example. He made his first solo flight in the minimum time. On first solo the student makes one circuit and landing only. His instructor then takes him up dual to review airwork, turns, climbing, gliding etc. and then sends him off solo to practise some. Now Magee was in the Junior course and had listened to the boys in the Senior course discussing their problems with aerobatics, loops, rolls, etc. So on his second solo flight he decided to do a roll. Minimum height for aerobatics was 3,000 feet above ground and so he climbed to 5,000 then 6,000 feet and feeling there was safety in altitude, which is true, he climbed to 8,000 and attempted his roll. Now, a Fleet Finch could slip into an inverted spin if stalled while upside down – this would not happen in a Tiger Moth, as they were very difficult to force into an inverted spin – but this could be classed as a fault or weakness in a Fleet. Magee entered an inverted spin when the blood rushes to the head and a pilot can 'red out', the opposite of a 'blackout' when the blood is drawn away from the brain. He struggled with the controls and finally pulled it out at about 600 feet above ground. Meanwhile, as he had been sent up for 30 minutes and almost an hour had gone by, his instructor became anxious and was watching for his return. On landing Magee bounced badly several times and taxied in to meet an irate A. K. Patterson. When Magee dismounted his steed, he was white as a sheet and shaking violently. He told A. K. what he had done and was taken to the

Medical Officer, who said, 'Take him right back up.' We were told that he shook for two days but recovered, and after a reprimand from the CO, continued his flying a wiser student.

John's own account of this nearly disastrous event was described in a letter to his parents on the evening of the 6th, immediately after it happened!

Do you know what a spin is? It is a horrid, sickening spiral dive towards the ground (ghastly and terrifying sensation) – in the last war they didn't know how to recover from them and consequently they took hundreds of lives. However, we do know now theoretically (full opposite rudder, stick back, then forward, and full throttle). Well, I asked my instructor if we could do one. He demurred, but I really wanted to, so we did. Soon I learned – or thought I learned – to do one myself (you can do one purposely to practise getting out of it), and he was very pleased, but warned me never to do one alone. That was yesterday. Last night I realized they had a sort of morbid attraction for me – possibly because they were so terrifying (N.B. the engine is off and all you hear is the wind screaming in the struts) – and today I was told to go to 3,000 feet and practise steep turns. On the way up a little devil kept telling me that I could easily do a spin if I got out of sight of the aerodrome, and nobody would be any the wiser. But it also taunted me for being afraid! I fought the thing during the long climb skywards, and finally in a fit of impatience decided to do one. So instead of levelling off as instructed, I continued climbing for 20 minutes until I was at the tremendous height of 6,500 feet, when I thought it safe to try, and let her go. As soon as I was in it I realized something was wrong. I had the feel of being slightly *upside down* yet still spinning. The ground was whirling before me when suddenly my safety belt snapped, and in the same moment I realized I was in an *inverted* spin, something I have only read of in heavy black type in flying manuals. My head hit the cockpit cowling and I came out of the seat. All the time I was hurtling like a corkscrew towards the earth. I had *no idea* how to get out of the thing. I applied full opposite rudder, but it made me spin all the faster. By this time my eyes were bulging out of my head and my ears blocked. I heaved on the control (joystick) column frantically but couldn't move it as I could not pull very hard with my safety belt bust. I think I became

unconscious then. The next thing I remember is making one last
effort and feeling myself pressed back into my seat as the nose came
up. I remember my altimeter needle trembling between 700 and 800
feet. I had dropped almost *5,000 feet* in about 20 seconds! As the ship
levelled out, I relapsed into a state of semi-fogginess, and when I
regained full use of my senses I headed straight for home but had
to circle the field twice before plucking up the guts to land. My
instructor came running out and started to give me a good going
over (he had watched the whole thing) but I was too dazed to listen.
But he climbed into the rear cockpit and took me straight up again
and immediately put me into two consecutive spins, later explaining
that, if he hadn't, I probably would never have been able to fly
again. When I finally staggered out of the plane, he put an arm
around my shoulder and said: 'Laddie, you've got what it takes.' I
am simply dreading that it will get to the ears of the C.O. as it
would be certain to wash me out. . . .

In spite of this, Alex Paterson remembered John 'as the finest pupil pilot
he taught to fly'. He certainly could not have forgotten him.[20]

On 23 February John successfully passed his 20-hour test, and the following
day began the next part of his training in aerobatics.

They are very exciting physically and leave you in a very low
condition. However, I am bearing up under this strain. I can now
loop the loop, do a slow roll, a half roll and loop out, a stalled turn,
a chandelle, and an Immelman. (The hardest manœuvre there is in
a low-powered ship – you go into a loop, and when on your back
at the top you roll out of it. If you aren't careful to have *exactly* the
right speed, you are liable to stall on your back and fall off into an
inverted spin.) These Immelmans are not actually on our course but
are a good thing to know in a tight corner. I have only done them
with my instructor; have not yet plucked up the guts to do one alone.
Aerobatics are very funny. You are apt to get a bit light headed and
it is a good thing to keep talking to yourself to keep 'on the ball' –
but they're marvellous, as you can imagine, for the thrill they give!
Flying upside down is queer. You hang in your safety belt and it's
very hard to keep your hands and feet on the controls. They tend
to fall off if you aren't careful. The rest of my 20 hours can be taken

up in aerobatics and cross-country flights to other aerodromes. Out of that will come about 5 hours instrument flying. I had 40 min. of this today – extraordinary sensation. We sit in the back cockpit, instead of the usual front, with a hood over our heads. Then you have to tell by your instruments exactly what is happening, how to correct it, etc. We have a Link Trainer here which has prepared us in part for this.

Within two weeks, on 5 March, John was delighted to pass his 50-hour test under the eagle eye of Flying Officer Vincent, the assistant Supervising Officer. Describing it the next day he wrote: 'He told me to do a snap half roll and loop out at 2,000 feet. Evidently wanted to see if I would do it (aerobatics are generally done at 6,000 feet). Tremendous thrill. . . .'

Today is a great day. Yesterday afternoon I successfully passed my 50-hour test, which took in aerobatics, and today I have just finished the last Ground School Exams. They were very hard, but I think I passed everything. I even got 67 per cent in Aero Engines, so when I get home you can rag me about having at last acquired a 'mechanical mind'!

Our Elementary Course is over. Quite a few who came here with us are 'Gone with the Wind' (that is, washed out), and the remainder, having gotten this far, should complete the course successfully and find Wings – and Action – at the other end of the road.

We have got through in record time, and the instructors seem to think we are quite an exceptional crowd. Accordingly, instead of going on leave, we are going to stay on here and take a course in Formation Flying, and Advanced Aerobatics, and will be practising actual combat among ourselves, probably with Camera Guns. We shall also be having Advanced Navigation in Ground School, Signals, Radio Direction Finding, etc. We are being 'guinea-pigged' – normally we would be going to Service School after some leave, but we are going to stay on here another month and put in another 50 hours flying, so that when we join Service Squadrons we will actually have some formation experience.

By 27 March the training was complete, the course was dismissed, and John, together with other successful trainees, returned to the Manning Pool at Toronto to await posting to Service Training Squadrons.

They were all very tired from the intensity of their training and under-nourished from the basic facilities that had been provided. Those who could afford it applied for weekend passes and booked into local hotels to 'sleep in respectable beds with springs. Last night I slept 15 hours.'

The wait was soon over, and John was posted to No. 2 SFTS Uplands, Ottawa, where on 10 April he began an intensive day of familiarization on a Yale trainer and within three days was learning to fly a Harvard. Gone were the frustrations, and the demand of the training occupied him completely.

You have no idea how fast, noisy, and generally terrifying these Harvards are. What thrills me is that planes of this type were actually used by the French against the Germans at Dunkerque. They have between eighty and ninety instruments as well as bomb-racks and machine guns (2) – though we usually carry camera guns for training purposes. I have not actually soloed in one yet, although I was ready to a week ago – the weather has always interfered. However, I have flown about ten hours solo on the Yale, an Intermediate trainer rather like the Harvard but without a retractable undercart with 360 instead of 600 horse-power engine.

He was now flying with men who were highly skilled and consequently not likely to be impressed by temperamental or erratic behaviour both in the air and on the ground. These exceptional Canadian instructors knew that the pilots they trained needed to understand and exploit the principles of aerobatics if they were to survive in future air battles.

'Height of attack and speed of dive' became a phrase common to everyday conversation, but the words needed to be actioned, and the instructors pushed their trainee pilots to the limits.

Yesterday I flew with my instructor, who is also our flight commander, up into the Gatineau Hills, North of Ottawa, about a hundred miles 'into the interior' as non-Canadians love to say . . . just about the most desolate spot I have ever seen. There he took over the controls and for forty-five minutes gave me the most thrilling low-flying exhibition I have ever dreamed of. Low flying in a Fleet was a thrill, but going 180 to 200 in a Harvard six inches off the ground (or water in this case) is really something. You haven't lived yet, poor earth-bound mortals! He flew between two rocks about ten feet apart and did three slow rolls in succession not more than eighty feet off the surface of the water (the best of fliers expect to lose a hundred feet in a roll). Just to the side of the lake was a big rocky mountain which we climbed in circles, then down went the nose and we flew vertically down a five hundred feet precipice, levelling off once more just over the water. I came the nearest to being air-sick I have yet in my aeronautical career!

John the daredevil who climbed a tree to save a kitten and used the clock tower at Rugby School as mountaineering training was still concealed in the formality of the polished shoes and buttons and a well-presented uniform. But he was never under total control, and pushing the boundaries or just being careless in situations with which he had limited experience were nearly his undoing. None of this appears in his log book, as he continued to satisfy the Uplands instructors with night and formation flying, instrument and safety tests, and he also completed 50 hours' flying and acquired his Mutual Instruction Certificate on 19 May.

With only a few more weeks of training ahead of him it could have been expected that with his goal within reach he would carefully follow the rules and keep out of trouble. But two incidents in close succession nearly ended his career. The first, described in his own words, was sheer bravado. The risks and excitement overruled the regulations.

I am in the dog house, I crossed swords with a pilot officer in our flight several weeks ago, and, having got his knife into me, he is screwing around in my back. He framed (actually, framed!) me on a charge a fortnight ago for which I lost half my prospects of a commission (which were, as I later discovered, the best in my class until that point, *mirabile dictu*). Today, however, a climax occurred when he followed, in a surreptitious manner, another chap and self, doing formation flying. After about 45 miles we broke it up for a breather and had a little dogfight. In came the P/O, whom neither of us recognized. So we ganged up on him and had a wonderful time.

Suddenly I recognised him and immediately disengaged, and left in a long diving turn for home, hoping he had not got my number. After a couple of minutes I looked around and, sighting a following aircraft, slowed down to 180 (from 275) and let him catch up, thinking I'd made a damn good getaway and this was my No. 2 coming back into formation. Needless to say it was the P/O, who got my number, did a couple of sarcastic pylon turns around me and left.

Now we are both on charge for:

1) Taking off in formation (which we didn't do, though we were quite close)

2) Not flying in formation all the time

3) Doing something else instead

4) To wit, unauthorized aerial combat

5) Driving an aircraft over 262 mph

6) Low flying at 700 feet, to which altitude he forced me down on disengaging.

God knows what will come of it all. One can only forecast with safety that I shall be barred from getting a commission and may very well be grounded for a month and set back a course or alternatively washed out altogether. But I have got to the point where I don't really give a damn anyway. I foresee weeks of C.B. [confined to barracks] ahead, which will be good, as I may get some studying done. After which we will dine together and I shall weep profusely as I tell you my troubles. . . .

Seriously, old man, I am most discouraged. I have tried like mad to keep my nose clean in this place, but it hasn't worked. My only consolation is that I am a cinch for the fighter command, which is my greatest desire! Heigh-ho!

Then there comes a moment of realization.

If that were all, things wouldn't be so bad, but Monday night I did something which affected also my reputation as a flyer, which has been unbelievably good to date, and was my one consolation. I misjudged a night landing and crashed on the runway, totally destroying a $35,000 aircraft but not even scratching myself. I was thrown clear (luckily my safety belt broke off) on the grass just off the runway. I don't think I have ever been so utterly mortified in my life. If I had hurt myself, I might have felt better about it! Then again it wouldn't have been so bad if (a) it hadn't been my fault and (b) if I hadn't been in the 'doghouse' already. But coming on the top of all that it sort of shattered me. It was early morning before I had pulled myself together enough to fill out all the accident reports and written a letter to the CO describing the accident (a local formality), and it was a very tired, angry, and thoroughly disgusted John Magee who crawled into bed just as the bugle was blowing in the morning.

I was grounded all yesterday and spent the rest of the day going from brass-hat to brass-hat and getting all the callings down you can imagine. I barely escaped getting on a charge again for my negligence in misjudging the flare-path. Suddenly I began to feel that something was wrong. I glanced at my air-speed indicator which read 85 m.p.h. Rather low, I thought (the Harvard's landing speed is 90 to 95 m.p.h.) and put my nose down a bit to gain the extra speed necessary. Then I couldn't figure out just how high I was. One's idea of elevation is not very good at night. A light looks the same at a hundred feet as it does at ten – at least as far as I can make out.

Suddenly I found out that I was practically on the ground and my immediate reaction was to pull the nose up. If I had remembered to hit the throttle I would have been O.K. but in the thrill of the moment I forgot it. The aircraft started up again and stalled about twenty feet off the ground. Immediately I lost control. A wing dropped and I dropped onto a wing-tip. There was a terrific jar, then I was thrown out of my seat as the plane cartwheeled around the wing-tip and dug her nose in, I landing on my face feeling very silly and angry. The plane looked so funny sort of grovelling around that I was almost tempted to laugh. Then all was still and I sat and swore silently for about a minute until a car came dashing out with the fire truck and ambulance behind it. It contained my own instructor, Flying Officer K, who happened to be Flying Control Officer for that night. He didn't know who it was and when I told him 'yes it's Magee', he gave a little laugh and said 'I might have known – you've certainly been having yourself a field day, haven't you?' Anyway he was so nice about it that I crawled into the back of the car and cried like a baby. I ought, I suppose, to be grateful for avoiding any black eyes, but I can't help feeling rather mortified that what started out to be such a promising career had to go and spoil itself like that. I think I was very lucky not to be washed out. At least I am still going to get my Wings.

So you see there's something in the old adage after all. It never rains but it pours!!

Now for my various offences I have three days C-B, seven days R-P [restricted privileges – no canteen, no late passes, and pack drill every day] and eleven days washing planes at the rate of two a day. It's a great life! I thought of applying for a week's leave to get rested up, but I don't want to impress them too much with the fact that I can't take it! I am passed fit for flying duties now, and am up again for night flying tonight. I should be frightened except for the fact that I've had so much bad luck that the law of averages, if nothing else, demands that I get a good break once in a while! Meanwhile Excelsior – Onward and Upward![21]

The Canadian instructors probably realized that, in spite of his intense training and his skills, John was still unreliable (he was still 18 and one month away from his 19th birthday). So he was allowed to take the different tests, which, if successful, would mean he could become a qualified pilot. He took his final Navigation test on 28 May, getting a score of 197 out of 200, the best in his group. He then achieved 98 out of 120 in Engines and Maintenance, second best in his group, and 91 out of 100 in Armament. Lastly on 3 June he completed his Instrument and Wings Test. He recalled that day in another letter.

'Magee was wanted for his Wings Test.' My heart fell to my boots, because everyone who flies knows that he can fly well one day and not the next. I was panic stricken as I know it was an 'off day' for me – and it was so hazy you couldn't see the ground from a thousand feet. And there was no horizon. However, I reported at the Flight room and found, to add to my despair, that I had drawn Flight Lieutenant S – who is accredited with being the toughest marker on the station. It was a very nervous I who climbed into a Harvard for the last time. It just happened that I got the highest standing in my Wings Test of all in our course except Steve.

So it all goes to show that you gain on the swings what you lose on the roundabouts. In a way I am rather glad that I didn't do well in Instruments, as they are inclined to make bomber pilots of the good instrument fliers. I think I am a cert. for a fighter pilot now but I shall not be getting a commission – at least for a while.

Yesterday 'Iron' Bill the C.F.I. [Chief Flying Instructor] (who is the toughest man I have ever run into in my life – and the squarest) asked us all what we wanted to do. I asked for Fighter Reconnaissance (Sea) Bomber, and Instructor, in that order. Of all the horrible things that could happen, being kept in Canada to instruct for the rest of the war is the most horrible that could happen to any of us. I am only afraid that my lucky high in my Wings Test may lead to my being made an instructor.

We are all through with everything now, and grounded too, as they have the strange idea that having won our Wings we might be inclined to play around too much in the air! Unfortunately we have to wait days for our Wings. We are ahead of schedule, but the Air Ministry has issued orders that we are not to have too long at home, as we might become too attached to civilian life! (N.B. UTTERLY RIDICULOUS J.G.M. JR.) Our course is scheduled to end on the 21st, and we will be sure of ten days leave as from then. However, we are going to make such nuisances of ourselves around this station if they try and keep us here till then that I can safely prognosticate that we shall be home considerably before then!

The words couldn't have been closer to the truth, and it seemed almost predestined that John would jeopardize his future career with another of his acts of wild bravado. In a letter to his brother David he recounted what happened.

I'm beginning to think that I'm being preserved for something big by the Fates especially after what happened today. I went with another chap on a solo cross-country flight to Mount Hope, another E.F.T.S. in Ontario. All the way there we did rolls, loops, Immelmans, stall turns, etc., and had one magnificent dog-fight (strictly against orders!), finally arriving about three quarters of an hour late. Got a going-over from the CO there and we took off for home. I was ahead, so looped over him and sat on his tail, about 50 yards behind, pouring imaginary tracers into him like the devil.

Suddenly, out of the blue, a Harvard dove down between us, just like a yellow blur. (They go about 200 to our 90.) The other chap went on home, but I stayed to grapple with the Harvard, despite the dis-advantage of speed and manoeuvrability. Needless to say he out-flew me all the time, but, whenever I got him turning around me, I could turn inside him and drill him. Finally I saw him coming down on my tail again, so I half rolled on to my back, and looped out, but held her in the dive till I had about 180 m.p.h. Pulled out at 500 feet, and, when my vision returned, he had already passed me and was circling a field. I circled inside but above him until he cut in and landed.

After taking a good look around (we would be washed out on the spot if caught), I landed too and taxied over to him. He turned out to be a Flying Officer from Dunville, where we hope to get eventually, and complimented me on keeping him in my sights as long as I did. Finally he started off again.

But there was a farmhouse at the windward corner of the field, so he decided to 'skim' it. This is another thing we are not allowed to do – that is, to fly low along the ground, then, almost in front of some fence, tree, etc., to yank back on the stick and zoom upwards at terrific speed. I did the same thing and, if he missed the house by five feet, I missed it by two. We climbed up and then dove on the unfortunate inmates again and again. Finally, I dipped my wings to him, thinking it was about time I got back. Besides, the ceiling was dropping rapidly and there was nasty looking weather to the N.W.

Imagine my plight when, arriving back at the aerodrome, I was told to report to the Chief Flying Officer's office immediately. I went there, shivering in my boots, to face both the CO and the C.F.I. [Chief Flying Instructor]. Apparently the poor benighted farmer had lodged a complaint against me, and what could I say in my own defence? Of course it was useless to plead engine trouble, as they obviously knew I had been deliberately 'low-flying', the greatest crime you can commit in this outfit.

I was quite open about it, told them about the whole thing, but refused to give the name of the Harvard pilot. Then the CO said he was probably going to wash me out, and went over to the Administration Building to see how I came out in our Ground School Finals, which had just been posted. I sat in silence with the C.F.I., who was just civil enough to offer me a cigarette.

Almost 10 minutes later the CO came back into the room, slapped me on the back, and said 'Sorry, Laddie, we haven't a hope of washing you out, you came in first!'

This really was fantastic news, as our subjects covered everything I've never been any good at – Aero engines, Armament, Navigation, Airframe Construction, Theory of Flight, Signals, Morse, etc., most of which I thought I'd flunked, so I escaped with the skin of my teeth.

His final words to me were: 'And for God's sake, remember that the crime is not in the doing, but in getting caught!'

John's log book records that all exercises were completed on 11 June and on the 16th he was awarded his Wings brevet. His instructor, Flying

Officer Alexander Paterson, sighed with relief as he bade him farewell, and it was not difficult for him in later years, when asked if he re-membered training John Magee, to smile and recall: 'He was the finest pupil pilot, amongst hundreds that I taught to fly – and the most spirited!! . . . He was destined to make his mark on the world for ever, but we would never have guessed how.'[22]

Chapter 6

Leaving Home

In June 1941 John wrote to his father, 'If I give up my life to fight evil, is that not exactly what you believe in and stand for?' [23]

With the training complete, it remained only for decisions to be made as to where and when John would be posted. It was with a huge sigh of relief that he was able to join his family in Washington DC and they were delighted to see him. John's father had clearly decided to settle down with his family in America and had been appointed Assistant Rector at the beautiful St John's Church in Lafayette Square in Washington.

All the family noticed how John had changed since the time they had been together at Martha's Vineyard. There were still excursions into the surrounding countryside, while he waited for his posting, but John was more composed in himself, quietly assertive and confident. His experiences in learning to fly and facing up to the real world had given him insight into his own talents and limitations.

> It isn't necessarily the most dashing hero who makes the best fighter
> pilot, it is the man who knows his machine, knows his enemy and
> above all knows himself. Knowing this, my limitations and how far
> I can go beyond the ordinary, I can be true to myself and to God.
> I want to fly with the best more than anything else in the world. [24]

Early in the morning of 1 July, a Western Union telegram arrived from Ottawa. It simply said: 'You have been appointed to the rank of Pilot Officer effective June 22.' His relief and delight, and pride mixed with anxiety, created a confused atmosphere around the last days of leave, as communications flashed to and fro with details of his posting to England, together with embarkation dates and times. So, having just become accustomed to being with his family, he experienced the heart-rending wrench of yet another parting. But, this time he was returning, in his own words, 'home, where I belong'. So John left his family and flew to Montreal, where the immediate involvement in preparation for em- barkation to England allowed little time for reflection. On 5 July 1941 John joined a large cohort of aircrew of either pilot officer or sergeant rank, all ambitious yet slightly anxious young men about to set sail for unknown experiences. The armed British merchant ship he boarded was named *California*, which in turn joined other ships such as the *Circassia* to make up a convoy bound for Iceland.[25]

'When I left —— on the —— I was on the water for two weeks before reaching —— where we spent a further fortnight on bully beef and sea biscuits and lost a good deal of weight.'[26] His letters were now subjected to security censorship and delayed in their delivery, so that the promises he had made to his parents about keeping them in touch with his pro- gress appeared to them to have been forgotten. This censored extract was from one of his letters that did not reach them until 2 March 1942, and they were worried because of the absence of news from him.

Apart from this correspondence, the only remaining accounts and information of the journey to England come from photographs taken en route and later recollections of other young men making the same journey. Hugh Russell and Turk Bailey were on the *Circassia*, while Terry Sassoon, Don Llewellyn and Jack Coleman were together on the *California*. Once they had disembarked in Iceland, there was little or nothing to do except wait to join another convoy. John, once again frustrated by the lack of action, deplored the waste of precious time 'just kicking our heels'.

One of the surviving photographs shows a group of men, including John, on a walking picnic in the hills somewhere near Thingvellir, and it was on such excursions that the hot springs, which were an unusual phenomenon, provided the novelty of daily shaving outdoors.

Eventually, having boarded another ship, they joined a second convoy, and three days later arrived in Greenock in Scotland. From Scotland the train journey south to England was slow and uncomfortable. It was packed with men, some of whom slept in the corridors.[27]

Then we took a boat from —— to —— and after a long and tedious train journey, in which we sat up twenty-four hours in a very cramped position (I slept on a luggage rack until it broke!), we arrived at the

Personnel Reception Center in —— and were put up in a
magnificent hotel for about a week, much to our astonishment.

They were located in Bournemouth, arriving on 31 July, and then dis-
tributed to different units for further training centres. John was posted to
Wales, to Llandow, No. 53 Operational Training Unit, and arrived there
on 5 August 1941. The very next day he began tests to determine his
suitability to learn to fly the highly manœuvrable and 'deadly Spitfire'.
On the 7th he had his first solo flight in the Spitfire and from that
moment was daily practising the amazing versatility of this aircraft. In
less than two weeks, on 18 August, he climbed to 33,000 feet and described it as the most exhilarating experience of his life. He wrote:

> I could rhapsodize for pages about the Spitfire. It is a thrilling and at
> the same time terrifying aircraft . . . it takes off so quickly that before
> you have recovered from the shock, you are sitting pretty at 5,000
> feet. Of course there is no telling what we will make of ourselves in
> this great game we have got into. Few of us, I imagine, have any
> idea as to what may lie ahead.[29]

Routine exercises were logged by John almost every day, weather permitting, and Mick Wilson, one of the leading instructors at Llandow,
remembered how John would 'hang around kicking his heels until the
cloud base lifted and he would always want to be the first away'.[30]

But, while routines of cloud flying, formation flying and astern attacks
were essential experience, the pages of his pilot's notebook that were most
heavily thumbed and annotated were at the centre of the manual: Stalling,
Spinning, Diving and Aerobatics. New words such as 'YAW' not only
became part of his daily vocabulary, but part of his 'trial and error'
experiences. Whenever he had the chance, he pushed the limits of his
own skill and the performance of the aircraft.

Never satisfied with being contained or restrained within limitations,
he was exhilarated and proud to lead the unit on 26 August to 26,000
feet. 'When you are there and surrounded by the azure blue, you don't
even hear the roar and throb of engines nor the buffeting of the slip-
streamed air – you are swept into an untrespassed space which is as for
ever. I sense a protected closeness to another power, a realization of the
wonder of his universe.'[31]

Writing to his parents on 3 September, he recounts having flown up to

30,000 feet, and it is certain that during the weeks at Llandow in mid-to late August he was inspired to write 'High Flight'. He sent the poem in another letter to his parents. 'I am enclosing a verse I wrote the other day. It started at 30,000 feet, and was finished soon after I landed. I thought it might interest you'.

High Flight
Oh! I have slipped the surly bonds of Earth
And danced the skies on laughter-silvered wings;
Sunward I've climbed, and joined the tumbling mirth
of sun-split clouds, – and done a hundred things
You have not dreamed of – wheeled and soared and swung
High in the sunlit silence. Hov'ring there,
I've chased the shouting wind along, and flung
My eager craft through footless halls of air. …

Up, up the long, delirious, burning blue
I've topped the wind-swept heights with easy grace.
Where never lark, or even eagle flew –
And, while with silent, lifting mind I've trod
The high untrespassed sanctity of space,
Put out my hand, and touched the face of God.

Elinor has had a novelette accepted by somebody or other, about which she is very excited. I go over where they are staying practically every day, but of late I have been spending most of my time in formation and air combat. I have heard definitely that our course here ends on the 13th of Sept so I expect to be on operations on the 20th. I think we are very lucky, as we shall just be in time for the autumn blitzes (which are certain to come).
If you get a chance, do see the following films.
Target for Tonight – British Ministry of Information
Dangerous Moonlight – about a Spitfire squadron
A Yank in the R.A.F. – (American)
Captain of the Clouds – This I think is a film made at Uplands in which I took part (formation, etc.)[32]
Flight Patrol – (American I think). Made with R.A.F. (?)
    All these films are relatively authentic and may give you some idea of what goes on in an operational squadron. The sort of things I

would not be able to describe in letters.[33]

Many men have claimed to be privy to the writing of 'High Flight'. Some assert that he read or recited it to them, others that they were witness to the act of its creation. None is reliable. John never put pen to paper and produced a poem at one sitting in the manner of writing a letter. The account of its creation in the letter to his parents – 'was finished soon after I landed' – describes what probably happened.

There are a variety of incomplete poetic descriptions of flight and flying from as early as January 1941. What happened was that John gradually built a poem as a result of high flying experiences, which then came into a final format. In this case 'High Flight'.

There was only one man, Pilot Officer J. R. Coleman, known as 'Jack', who was likely to have known about the creation of 'High Flight'. He was four years older than John and hailed from Hampton, New Brunswick. His maturity and generosity occasionally had a calming influence over his ebullient friend. Of the poem Jack recalled: 'I watched it grow in him and although it chopped and changed, he knew when it was done and as we walked the airfield in driving Welsh rain, he recited it from start to finish. I put my arm around him when it was over and just held him; he knew I knew!'

Chapter 7

Elinor and Rugby

In his letter to his parents on 3 September 1941, John commented about news of Elinor and her excitement about the possible publication of a novelette she had written. He is longing to see her. When he left England in the summer of 1939, John had parted from his dearest love and the security given to him by the Lyon family. But all of Elinor's family loved John. Now back in England, the words in the poem 'Prospect', which he had written especially for Elinor, describe his true feeling for her.

Prospect
I know, dear heart, that some day I shall find you
Alone, and in the evening shade of trees;
Twilight, and hills, and quietness behind you
A scent I shall remember in the breeze . . .

Always you come, a precious ghost, to haunt
The days, the nights; – in sudden, waking dreams
I find your face; you smile, you beckon; – flaunt
Your lovely self before my eyes; it seems

To love is pain! But did you really care?
Have you forgotten? – Is it all in vain
To breathe out sonnets to the midnight air,
To long to touch your hands, your lips again?

And yet, I know that some day I shall find you
Alone, and in the evening shade of trees;
Twilight, and hills, and quietness behind you
A scent I shall remember in the breeze. . . .

Elinor had been in contact with John during his time in America. Letters had crossed the Atlantic too from Hugh Lyon, who, even at such a distance, proffered advice and guidance to John's exasperations and frustration. Just as he had guided John at school and taken him into his family, so, when John returned, he still maintained his support and watched the relationship develop with Elinor with admiration. In January 1939 Elinor left home and went to school in Switzerland, returning in late summer to Rugby, before taking up her place in the autumn at Lady Margaret Hall, Oxford University, to study English. John, meanwhile, had left for America with his friend Dermott, and he had consequently missed Elinor at Rugby.

John's parents had been astonished by the number of John's girlfriends – one he even declared he would marry![34] But once he had left home for England on board the *California* he forgot them and his thoughts turned back to Elinor. His parents forwarded a letter of Elinor's, and he replied to them: 'Thank you for sending E's letter, which I must have left behind. I was looking frantically for it only a few days ago. I find that the prospect of seeing her again this summer has a lot to do with my anxiety to get home!'

John announced his return to England to the Lyon family by taking an unauthorized flight south to Gloucestershire, where Elinor and her family were staying with friends on a farm. He flew low over the field where they were picking fruit, ascending rapidly and, climbing through a tight circuit, buzzed the sleepy village and then landed in a nearby field. Hugh Lyon recalled the day: 'He was on top of the world. All the poet adventurer in him found outlet and expression in the Air Force.'

Less than a week later he was showing off again and fully aware of the regulations he was flouting.

The other day I was lucky enough to get a Spit without any squadron markings on it, so I could fly as low as I liked and not get turned in. First of all, I beat up the Lyons for about three-quarters of an hour, almost touching the grass on the tennis court several times. After that, I shot off to S   and beat up Dermott, then down to Mortehoe to have a look at Granny.[35] Unfortunately, at the top of the hill I misjudged a pull-out and left some elevator fabric on a bramble bush. Must have given her quite a thrill, but it took some explaining back here.

Training at Llandow came to an end on 13 September. John and Jack waited for their postings, hoping they could remain together. They had several days' leave and stayed with Dermott at his parents' house, their stay being recorded in the visitors' book. As Dermott remembers, John celebrated the event by marking it in a way that only he could: 'He flew over the house and woods so low that the slipstream rocked the tops of the trees. He was of course upside down!'

Elinor was also subjected to aerobatics in the same week: 'He went to it in the full and almost joyful knowledge of the hazards which went with it, especially to one who, like himself, did not know the meaning of "safety first"!'

In calmer mood he walked with Elinor on Bredon Hill, a day that Elinor later recalled in a poem. She found, 'he was just like his letters, full of life and ready to enjoy everything that happened to him pleasant or not. . . . I think it made him happy to see England again, we talked very cheerfully and raced each other downhill.'

With only a few days left of his leave, he was back and forth to see Elinor and her family. She recalled that, apart from his showmanship visits in a Spitfire, 'he did come more prosaically by train and brought us some American nylons, which were like gold in those days. My mother said, "Don't you want to give these to your best girl?" to which he replied, "You're my best girls", meaning her, my sister and me.'

John regarded the three of them as his family, and Elinor recalled how her mother, and perhaps her father as well, considered him as their adopted son: 'My brother, their son, died when he was 14. He had a faulty heart and I think, you know, she always regretted not having a son who was all right.'[36]

On 16 September John had received his posting to RAF Digby in Lincolnshire. He had no idea where Digby was, and on arrival at the base with Sergeants Pearce, Graham and Thomson, he recalled how friendly a place it was: 'It was a truly amazing lot to join. They made us feel so welcome. Any excuse for a party is good enough.' But he had come to fly, and in his usual manner he was quick to be back in the air. 'I have spent all day dog fighting and feel exhausted. Most of it was at 20,000 feet, where oxygen is needed. I felt like Icarus about to singe his wings. Incidentally, I have been as high as 33,000 feet, higher than the top of Mount Everest.'[37]

In spite of these achievements, which were exciting in their own right, it is clear from John's own records and the Digby Operations Record Book that on arrival he was also assessed for his flying capability and then given several days' dual instruction with his Squadron Leader, Rob Davis, and then Flying Officers with equal experience, Adams and Bollard. The touches of brilliance recognized by his instructor at Llandow now needed to be underpinned by the discipline required in formation flying by day or night.

By early October the weather on the east coast of Lincolnshire began to turn towards winter and the practice that was needed became more irregular. Always willing to help out, John was chosen to act as a kind of test pilot for some of the older aircraft on the station.

Recently I have been acting as test pilot for the squadron. We have one old kite that is in the last stages of decrepitude, which nobody likes to fly. It had a thorough overhaul but they didn't manage to get the wheels quite right, so, in a rash moment, I volunteered to air-test it. Everything went all right until I came in for a landing, and then the wheels wouldn't come down. The only thing you can do in such a case is to go through a series of short dives and violent pull-outs, which is pretty hard on the pilot and very hard on the wings!

I went round and round the aerodrome very low doing this until I thought the wings would come off, but still they wouldn't come down. I was almost ready to crash-land it, with the wheels retracted, when I decided to have one more go. I got up to about 2,000 feet (I couldn't get it to climb properly as the engine was not running at all well), rolled onto my back and chopped vertically onto the aerodrome. I held it as long as I dared – and a little longer – then hauled the stick back into my stomach as hard as I could. All I remember before blacking out was a very violent jerk and shudder which I mentally noted as the disappearance of the wings (a most essential part of any aeroplane!) but when I came to again my impressions were chronologically as follows:
i. The wings are here
ii. The wheels are down
iii. I am about to hit a hangar

However, I finally got down safely. On taxiing up to the flight officer, I found – you'll never guess – the Duke of Kent inspecting the squadron. My Flight Commander introduced me and said 'Nice work', which I took as an enormous compliment, as he is not exactly given to flattery. The Duke had watched the whole procedure and seemed duly impressed. . . .[39]

Today I tested the same aircraft again. The mechanic had been onto it and guaranteed that it would work, so I took off gaily in the direction of my old school [he is referring to Rugby], which I duly found, and, the plane having no markings on it [it had just been repainted], proceeded to give the old place a really good 'beating up'. I had fleeting impressions of boys pouring out of classrooms; Barbara Lyon waving a blue handkerchief; Eric Reynolds standing aghast by his bicycle; and that hideous monstrosity, the school chapel.

Having arrived back at the aerodrome I found once more that the wheels stuck. So, mouthing words at the flight mechanic, I started to go through the same manœuvres as before. This time I had a little more height and could afford to be more violent. After 45 minutes I got them down at the expense of two engine cowlings, the hood and several bolts out of the wing-roots, which all shook off in the process. I have just told the engineering officer that next time I'm going to bail out and let it fall into the sea!

I don't know why I should have spent two pages telling you of such a mundane article as an undercart, but news is rather scarce.[40]
P.S. I have decided to be a flying instructor after the war. If it looks like ending suddenly, please get me a job at once!
P.P.S. I like flying.[41]

While trying to get aircraft back into service was a useful pastime, it was not going to win the war. Not surprisingly, with many of the Canadian pilots and ground crew standing waiting for the weather to improve or aircraft to be available, rationalization was needed.

With the arrival on station of a flight of new Spitfires, Mark Vb, more heavily armed than its predecessor with four .303 machine guns and two 20mm canons, 412 Squadron moved to a nearby satellite airfield at Wellingore.

A landing ground at Wellingore first came into use in mid-1917, when aircraft of the Royal Naval Air Service from nearby Cranwell started to use it. In early 1940 a proper grass aerodrome was established as a satellite of Digby, and the first aircraft to arrive were the Bristol Blenheim fighters of 29 Squadron, which moved from Digby on 8 July. The squadron then started to convert to the Bristol Beaufighter in September and carried out its first operation with the new type on 17 December. Conversion was completed in full by February 1941, and the squadron moved to West Malling in Kent at the end of April; one of 29 Squadron's pilots during this period was Flight Lieutenant Guy Gibson, later famous as the leader of the 'Dambusters' raid.

Digby was transferred to Canadian control, and 402 (RCAF) Squadron arrived at Wellingore in May, but was replaced by the Spitfires of 412 (RCAF) Squadron, transferring on 20 October 1941.

Chapter 8

Wellingore: Administrative HQ

By nightfall the new Spitfires, their pilots and ground crew had been transferred to a muddy grass field outside the village of Wellingore. As their precious new fighters were locked down for the night, the pilots and ground crew made their way across the airfield to their Mess and sleeping accommodation. The village was surrounded by newly created airfields, which were rapidly being brought into service to cope with the ever-increasing demand for fighters and bombers to attack the enemy.

In the centre of Wellingore village was a large hall, which had been requisitioned early in 1940. It provided an ideal centre for the new squadrons arriving from Canada. The following is the only surviving account of how this took place.

The Squadrons were to occupy Wellingore Hall as their Administrative HQ, as it was conveniently situated for nearby satellite airfields. Until the domestic accommodation was built, they would also reside therein, as it was a huge building. My first task was to arrange for all furniture and moveable equipment to be removed from the hall into the custody of a local Estate Agent, and to catalogue all such items. This proved to be a most interesting experience.

The Hall had remained unoccupied since before World War I and at first sight was reminiscent of the scenes from the film of Charles Dickens's *Great Expectations*. The wallpaper was peeling from the walls. Enormous cobwebs were festooned all over the place, which had been shuttered for twenty-five years or so. Most of the heavy curtains had rotted at the windows. In the huge library, hundreds of books were mouldering on the shelves. The vast kitchen was a heartbreaking sight with its rusting equipment, particularly the large coal-fired ranges literally red with rust. In the outbuildings was a 1908

Daimler Benz motor car and also a complete chemistry laboratory and photographic darkroom with some partly developed glass plate pictures. Inside the house, one large drawing room had been fitted out as an engineering workshop and the lathes were still there, covered in grime and rust.[43]

I cannot now recall the name of the owner of the house but I gather from the local gossip that he was an inventive genius. The story goes that just prior to World War I he worked with a German assistant chemist. As a result of their experiments, they discovered the formula to produce aniline dyes, which I gathered were the first really successful permanent dyes. The owner left for Lincoln the next morning and caught a train to London to patent the discovery. Upon arriving at the Patent Office, he learned that his so-called partner had already filed the patent earlier that day, having travelled to London the previous evening for this purpose. It appears that this perfidy unhinged his mind and he never returned to Wellingore Hall. One other of his inventions was a sprinkler system as a method of fire fighting. The flat roof of the Hall had been converted into what was, in effect, a huge swimming pool, which was lead lined. This caught any rainfall. The water could be gravity fed through valves in the ceiling of each room or corridor, should the occasion arise.

Within a fortnight, the Hall had been cleared, cleaned and made habitable. Even the kitchens achieved some of their original pristine glory. The Canadians moved in and the construction of the two satellite airfields continued apace and by early August were completed, and with them my task. I enjoyed my brief stay with the Canadians and being the only Englishman on the site was something of a novelty.[44]

The Hall was crammed with more than 400 men, mostly Canadians, all of whom needed to eat, sleep and be entertained. The overspill of ground crew and non-commissioned men was packed into tents in the Hall grounds, while officers were secreted away in a large house close by, known as The Grange, which accommodated about twenty officers sharing rooms. John paired up with P/O Bob Edwards. The cheek-by-jowl existence suited John well enough, with his familiarity with close-proximity living. So routines were quickly established and, weather permitting, Flights A and B interchanged throughout flying hours, gaining all the competences needed not only to survive, but to win.

Chapter 9

Leave with Elinor

As the month came to an end, John had seven days' leave and set out again to find Elinor. By coincidence, Dermott Magill was also a student at Oxford at Oriel College, and their reunion at Oxford rail station was memorable in so many ways.

The arrival of the train was scheduled for midday. Dermott, having overslept, rushed to be on time to join Elinor at Oxford station. On seeing John alight from the train, Dermott hurried forward, leaving Elinor. Clasping John's hand he greeted him excitedly. 'And how's Maggie? It's so good to see you!' They hugged each other and then suddenly became conscious that in their delight they had ignored Elinor who was standing to one side, quietly amused. Realizing their mistake they immediately embraced her and the three of them held each other tightly. Standing back to admire Elinor, John commented on the academic gown she was wearing. 'I was determined to wear it to impress you,' she replied. 'And I came to show you my officers' dress uniform, not that casual flying gear I was wearing when I last saw you,' John responded.

Elinor later recalled[45] that she had felt somewhat embarrassed at not realizing how close they were to each other – like brothers. Then she added: 'But they had shared a room together at Rugby, so it was quite natural.' As they walked from the station, the joking between the two men was relaxed and ebullient, but Elinor eventually jostled between them and announced: 'We're not going to call you Maggie, I don't like it and it doesn't suit you.'

'But I was only saying it because he [pointing to John] told me in his last letter that all the officers in Lincolnshire call him Maggie.'

'Well we're not doing it,' said Elinor. 'If you don't want to be John, you'll have to be what your aunts called you, "Ian", so as not to get you confused with your father.'

John intervened, stopping and turning her towards him: 'I want to be who you want me to be and there is no one who knows me better than you.'

She looked at her tall and elegant officer, immaculately presented and sporting his recently grown moustache. 'All right,' she said, 'Dermott and I will introduce you to all our friends as John, John our best friend ever', and she kissed him lightly on the cheek, smiling. The three of them walked on to the Porter's Lodge of Elinor's college, where they parted company with arrangements to meet up later.

The place, the company, the continuous chatter among Dermott's friends all gave John the thrill of new experiences, with which he was totally at ease; he was in his element. There were long discussions late into the night, which later Dermott recalled as

> being as if we were in our tiny cell-like room in Rugby. John just poured his heart out and it was obvious he wanted to be in Oxford for many reasons, not least of which was due to his reawakening as to how much he loved Elinor. There were so many things I now remember. We found him a spare gown, got him out of his uniform and took him to a lecture. I think it was on Goethe. He couldn't get enough of it. We managed to stop him asking questions at the end, but for hours afterwards he wouldn't stop discussing the pros and cons of it – he even made some notes on an envelope. He was just like the John back at school – so sharp – so so clever.

Next day Elinor served afternoon tea for John in her room at Lady Margaret Hall. It was a unique occasion for them both – alone together with time to be themselves. A visit to the theatre followed, John, Dermott and one of his friends accompanying Elinor and two of her friends. They went to see an opera called *The Blue Goose*.[46] John and Elinor managed to arrange to sit next to each other and paid little attention to the drama. John recalled later that they were chattering most of the time; then the theatre was followed by supper at a restaurant. As he later wrote to his parents:

> Then we walked the girls back to L.M.H. On the way, one of the other girls walked with me, but Elinor rather skilfully edged her out by stumbling more or less between us. I would give my eyes to know if that stumble was really an accident.[47] I ought to be able to get down to see Elinor more often. She has really turned out to be the most

inspiring girl. I enjoy her company more now than ever before. . . .
Really I think she must be the girl for me. But I foresee years of hard
work before I win her heart! Any advice will be gratefully received.[48]

Recalling the Oxford visit many years later, Elinor remembered how
John still seemed extraordinarily young. She thought that he must have
realized this, because 'he had grown a moustache and started to smoke
a pipe to appear more manly!' Elinor was older, more mature and cautious,
and had always regarded John as too young for her to take seriously with
all his romantic ideals.

She had a true affection for him, though, and when he visited Oxford,
she intentionally concealed from him that she had another regular
boyfriend, Peter Wright.[49] 'It was not the right time to tell him and it would
have created another crisis for us both in what were very uncertain times.'

Leaving Oxford, John paid his grandmother a quick visit at Mortehoe
in Devon, and then quickly returned to Wellingore. He had purchased a
well-worn second-hand motorbike and had left it with Jim Hartland, his
batman at the Officers' Mess in The Grange, who, as a trained mechanic, 'sorted it out in his spare time'.

A second trip to Oxford on the restored machine was fast and erratic. In
spite of the time spent repairing it, John had difficulty starting and re-
starting it. He arrived at Oxford on Saturday, 26 October, in improvised
motorcycle clothing, which Elinor remembered

> was probably what he wore for flying . . . he looked very dashing but
> it was a very short visit. Then we said goodbye. Looking back it was
> a strange moment. He didn't want to go and I didn't want him to.
> I wanted to hug him and hold him but we shook hands rather
> solemnly. Words didn't come easily, it seemed rather foolish and
> inadequate to wish him good luck – I said something like 'take care'
> and moments later, 'be safe'. He started his motorbike, he waved,
> I was nearly crying. The motorbike cheered us up a bit. It went five
> yards and stopped dead. We laughed, he shrugged his shoulders and
> started it again, he waved his hand and was gone round the corner.
> I stood for some time, tears in my eyes, wondering, wishing, as I
> have many times since, that I'd never said 'take care'. I just wanted
> someone, some greater power to look after him. Of course it was
> my suggestion that he should call in at Rugby on his way back to

Wellingore, as I knew my parents would be glad to see him.

The journey to Rugby was without mishap and Elinor's father, Hugh, recalled:

> He arrived late one night and, just before he went back the next afternoon, he came and talked a little to me as I was sawing wood in my garage. It was good of him to come round, for he was in a hurry. He spoke a little about my family, a little about the prospects of going abroad, but not much about anything. It wasn't necessary somehow. 'So in all love we parted.' After he had gone, I went on sawing and thinking of him and the fine man he was growing up to be.

That night, in her rooms in Lady Margaret Hall, while John roared through the night back to Lincolnshire, Elinor captured her deepest thoughts and emotions of the day:

> A milky phosphorescence hangs
> Above the apple trees,
> Pale as the gleam that haunts the foam
> At night, in shallow seas.
> Shepherds made love in Arcady
> Beneath such boughs as these.
>
> The plough bestrides the heavenly field
> Beyond the ancient hill;
> Like nameless flowers of the night
> The stars hang clear and chill;
> Below them, in benighted hearts
> All mortal fires are still.
>
> Till day revive their dreaming flame.
> Let human longings sleep;
> The apple-blossom gleams, the trees
> Stand in enchantment deep;
> And all above, a million stars
> Eternal vigil keep.

The next day, 30 October 1941, John was flying again, practising air combat and taking an endurance test. It was on the following weekend

that he wrote to one of his girlfriends in Canada, Mimi, enclosing a
poem in which he said he had been trying to 'capture the inspiration of
flight'. Mimi kept the poem as her secret for many years and only later
in her life did she make it available for others to enjoy.

> **Oh Once Again**
> To climb aloft and watch the dawn ascend
> Earth's haze-enshrouded rim. To dally high
> And see the morning ghosts forsake their blend
> For sundry silhouettes. To catch the sky
> Transformed, its fawn and silv'ry tints now rife
> With brilliant hues recast. To ease my craft
> Below as golden darts give birth to life
> And set the world astir. To catch a shaft
> Of beaming warmth, and quickened by its touch
> Assault its course through hills of airy fleece.
> To burst at last above the crests and clutch
> The fleeting freedom – endless blue, at peace.[50]

Chapter 10

Close to the Edge

On Wednesday, 5 November, John took off from Wellingore at 10.30 a.m., together with Sergeant Macdonnell and Sergeant Linton from 'A' Flight and Sergeant Backhouse and Pilot Officers Denkman and Smith from 'B' Flight. All were to engage in Height Climbing, which may have become quite competitive once they were in the upper air, away from the airfield. John took his aircraft to 36,000 feet, encountering problems with oxygen control – his aircraft, known as 'Brunhilde',[51] performed exceptionally well but crashed on landing. Photographs of the fractured aircraft suggest that John was careless when landing, and the accident report, completed by Squadron Leader Bushell on the same day, confirms that the aircraft AD329 VZ-B was badly damaged.[52]

The report profile 2(a) asks for extracts from the Officer Training Unit report, and the only extract quoted is: 'Shows patches of brilliance. Tendency to over confidence 53 OTU.' Section 2(b) asks for the opinion of the Station Commander as to the suitability of the pilot for retention in a fighter squadron. Squadron Leader Bushell simply writes: 'I recommend that pilot be kept in squadron.'

November was beginning to be a busy month for the squadron and its flying confidence was tested in many different ways. The war with Germany, particularly over the Channel and northern France, was unrelenting, and 412 Squadron was needed further south. Young men with limited experience found themselves leading flights of aircraft into attack, and on Saturday, 8 November, Squadron Leader Bushell led two flights into battle, with John as one of the pilots. This combat report from one of those involved is an authorized account of what took place:

No. 412 (R.C.A.F.) Squadron was ordered to WEST MALLING on 8/11/41 to take part in circus operation No. 110 over the French

Coast. 12 Spitfire Vb's took off at 0845 hours and landed at WEST
MALLING at 0935 hours. No. 412 Squadron took off from WEST
MALLING at 1117 hours in company with No. 616 Squadron and 411
(R.C.A.F.) Squadron, the wing being led by WING COMMANDER SCOTT.
The Wing were over MANSTON at approx. 1135 hours at 18,000 feet
and gained height over the Channel with the Squadron stepped
down into the sun at intervals as follows: 412 Squadron in sections of
four flying in vic formation at 23,000 feet, 411 Squadron at 21,000
feet and 616 Squadron at 20,000 feet. The Wing reached the French
Coast N.E. of Dunkirk in this formation at approx. 1145 hours but in
view of the fact that this was earlier than the ordered time of 1152
hours, the Wing carried out a sharp left hand orbit, and proceeded
to patrol the coastline N.E. of Dunkirk where a heavy and accurate
barrage of A.A. was encountered which split up the Wing
formation. The Wing did not reach the patrol line East of Dunkirk.

After we had been on patrol for about 20 minutes, I lost the Wing
while watching vapour trails of two Me. 109s about 300 feet above.
When I discovered I was alone, I dived down to sea level and flew
towards the coast of England. About 10 miles N.W. of Dunkirk I saw
a Me. 109E at about 200 feet, about a quarter of a mile to my right.
I turned to attack, thinking to surprise him from below but the pilot
saw me and turned towards me. We sparred round in tight turns at
sea level for about a minute and then the Me. broke off suddenly
and made for the French coast. By the time I had straightened out
and was in good position astern for a shot, he was about 300 yards
range. I gave a 3-second burst of cannon and machine guns where-
upon black smoke began to stream from his engine. Another Spitfire
then passed to the left closing quickly on the E/A which was
apparently the reason for his breaking off the fight so suddenly. The
E/A waggled its wings as if the pilot was hurt and unsteady on the
controls. By that time we were quite near the French coast with the
Me. still under control. I gave another very short burst at about 500
yards range with no visible effect and I turned and made for England
along with the other Spitfire, but I could not get close enough to see
his Squadron markings. I landed at Manston at about 1300 hours.
Rounds fired: 20mm 36 .303 144.

John's own account of the baptism by fire is contained in several letters,
and the following extracts reveal his response to events:

November 10, 1941. I have at last been in action. November 8th I shall never forget. I can't tell you much about it, but it took place in enemy territory. I was flying in the leading section of four as the C.O.'s wing man. We were jumped and I was the only one to avoid getting hit. The C.O., who used to be my Flight Commander, a Pilot Officer, and our best sergeant were all shot down.

He had only had his stripes up for one day when he led the Squadron, and was shot down. I was the last man to see him alive, as, just before we took off, he was giving me a little fatherly advice, as it was my first action and I was a little uneasy. I flew as his wing man.

We were jumped by four 109s who picked one of us each. We all turned into them immediately, but I turned so violently that I spun down a good many thousand feet and got away. The other three were all shot down. I saw D—— go straight into the sea. P—— tried to bail out, but his parachute didn't open. Nobody saw what happened to Kit, but we all think and hope he is a prisoner of war. He was one of the grandest men I have ever known.

It was when I was way below the others that I got my squirt. A 109 was following somebody down, firing intermittently and all I had to do was turn in behind and fire at him, but another one pulled the same trick on me, and, when I saw tracers going by, it was time to forget about my bird, who, I think, must have got it as he was a sitting target for me. However, I couldn't claim him, as I didn't see him go in.

I have described what happened on one sweep. We shall be doing more and more of these in the future. Once you get over your fear at the 109s you get to love it. We are also doing low flying cannon attacks on aerodromes, power plants and other such targets. They're great fun but the anti-aircraft fire is a little disconcerting at first. . . .

His log book notes: 'Shot at ME 109E. Kit, Denk and Pick missing.' The Operations Record endorses John's comments: 'Squadron Leader Bushell (Kit) – Missing; Pilot Officer Denkman (Denk) – Missing and Sergeant Pickell (Pick) – Missing.' Now faced with the stark reality of warfare, he turned again to his mastery of language to find words to express his real feelings. Grounded by bad weather, 'No Flying Weather u/s' on Monday, 10 November, he included in his letter home another poem. He called the poem 'Per Ardua'. *Per ardua ad astra* is the motto of the Royal Canadian Air Force. Under the title, he introduced the poem with:

To those who gave their lives to England during the
Battle of Britain and left such a shining example to us
who follow, these lines are dedicated.

They that have climbed the white mists of the morning;
They that have soared, before the world's awake,
To herald up their foemen to them, scorning
The thin dawn's rest their weary folk might take;

Some that left other mouths to tell the story
Of high blue battle, – quite young limbs that bled;
How they had thundered up the clouds to glory
Or fallen to an English field stained red;

Because my faltering feet would fail I find them
Laughing beside me, steadying the hand
That seeks their deadly courage –
Yet behind them
The cold light dies in that once brilliant Land . . .

Do these, who help the quickened pulse run slowly,
Whose stern remembered image cools the brow –
Till the far dawn of Victory know only
Night's darkness, and Valhalla's silence now?

Compared to the delight and joy of his previous poem, 'Oh Once Again', this poem reflects a more sombre mood and was inspired by the tragic loss of his close comrades. 'I am not particularly anxious to have it printed unless you think it vital to the conduct of hostilities. Seriously, though, do use it for any purposes such as War Relief, etc.'

He concludes his letter by telling his parents,

Really I am loving the whole thing. Incidentally, when we go on these operations across the Channel, we usually fly down as a Squadron to —— or some other field and refuel and then go across from there. After the sweep on the 8th (my first) I landed at —— but everyone was sent back again to look for survivors in the sea. It was dark when I got back and I spent the night there and then flew back here the following morning feeling rather enervated. I passed very low over Foxburrow, which seemed to be intact. On these sweeps you go over as a Squadron, but you invariably get split up and dribble back in twos and threes and land at the first aerodrome you can find. We are expecting to move down south any time now – and the fun will really begin. There will be operations every day instead of once or twice a week, as here. Actually we have been putting in a great deal of practice flying up here – particularly at night. I am well on the way to being night-operational. As soon as we have two dozen pilots night-operational, we will be allowed to take part in night-flying activities too. . . . You must imagine me doing a little more as the weeks go by (it's all a matter of experience) and, incidentally, having the time of my life![53]

The squadron needed time to regroup and work together to improve its air attack tactics – it also needed to get used to its rapidly changing personnel. As soon as a man was reported missing from an operation, his bed was taken by another.

Kit Bushell's death left another problem, his dog. The loyal Alsatian called 'Czar' would not let anyone touch any of Kit's possessions and guarded his bed for days until another officer tempted him away with left-over scraps of meat from the kitchen. The dog then became attached to John's friend, Rod Smith, and slept under his bed for a time, until Dusty Davidson, another Canadian Pilot Officer befriended it.

Kit had been Squadron Leader only a few days and had had his stripes for one day – it had been on his signature that John had remained with the squadron and was still permitted to fly after crashing 'Brunhilde'. It was also Kit who, just before take-off, had recognized John's nervous anticipation and had given him some fatherly advice. Now that Kit had been killed in action, John was more acutely aware of the fine line between life and death.

Grey low cloud now moved in from the east, which grounded aircraft and left men isolated from their daily routines. Weather testing and exercises such as rehearsing a scramble filled a few hours, but it was fortunate that another diversion occurred to break the monotony of waiting.

Chapter 11

Royal Visit

On Thursday, 13 November, the official Operations Record recalls, 'in spite of inclement weather, the Squadron was honoured with a visit from His Majesty King George VI. He was accompanied by Air Marshal Sir W. Sholto Douglas C-in-C Fighter Command, Air Vice-Marshal R. E. Saul AOC No. 12 Group, Air Commodore L. F. Stevenson AOC, RCAF in Great Britain, Colonel Lascelles (Equerry), Group Captain P. Campbell OCRAF, Digby and Wing Commander Fielding ADC, Captain King's Flight, were in attendance. His Majesty chatted with all the pilots and numerous other ranks during his tour of inspection and afterwards attended informal tea in the Dispersal hut.'

Squadron Leader Morrison, who had been promoted to squadron commander only the day before, guided the Royal Party off the main road called Pottergate and down a farm track towards Wellingore airfield. The sketch maps drawn later by men and officers who took part show that the Parade Ground was in front of a farmhouse.[54] The purple Royal Daimler moved slowly through inches of mud and was held up in its progress by ducks and geese.[55] The parade took place with due ceremony in spite of the drizzle and low cloud, and then the official party walked to a nearby dispersal hut. The national press photographers were excluded from this informal venue, but RCAF photographers were in the hut and recorded this unique event. Written accounts that have survived give an insight into what took place.

All the pilots (including sergeant pilots) and four officers gathered in the dispersal hut, but Pilot Officer Needham and the Intelligence Officer Hart Massey had decided to miss the parade and hid in the hut, only to be caught out when the Royal Party arrived.

For some reason or other, Hart and I avoided going on parade that

day and we holed up in the dispersal hut all cuddled up in Irwin
flying jackets to keep warm. As far as I know the King's visit to the
dispersal hut was not on the agenda, otherwise we would not have
been there. First thing I knew, King George and entourage arrived
at the dispersal hut, Hart and I scrambled to our feet and I slunk
into the background, while Hart extended his hand and greeted his
majesty. Of course, Hart was well known, having been cox for
Oxford and also the son of Canada's High Commissioner.[56]

Sergeant Joe Cassidy remembers that 'the photographers had chased the
ducks onto the parade ground for a gimmick . . . when speaking to some
of the young pilots later, they were quite shocked at his [the King's] 'salty'
language. The poor chap was just trying to be one of the boys.'[57]

Whatever was said, Rod Smith recalls John Magee confidently standing talking to the King, who would have been surprised to meet a Canadian pilot with a polished English accent. Clearly the event impressed
John, another highlight, and he tore out a copy of the parade photograph, marked those who could be identified, and on 3 December sent it
to his parents.

P.S. F/L Chuck Cantrill 'B' Flt. commander Lt Comdr has gone
abroad, as has F/L Bob Edwards, my erstwhile roommate. F/L Bill
Archer is now 'A' Flt. Comdr in Kit Bushell's place. Our new
commanding officer, Jack Morrison, is an absolute prince. I am
a section leader now and for some time have been second 'i/c of
a Flight'. Excelsior! I almost forgot to thank you for my November
check. I hope to be able to cut down on this soon, but will let you
know. At the moment we are listening to Lord Hawhaw, who is not
well received in this Mess but we listen regularly for news of those
we have lost.

In the enclosed pictures (of our squadron being reviewed by the
King)
1 Chuck Cantrill, Acting CO – it was soon after Kit went.
2 Mel
3 H.M.
4 Air Marshal Sir Sholto Douglas – C in C Fighter Command.
5 Group Captain Campbell, Station Commander. NOTE THE MUD!

The weather records for November show it to have been grey, overcast, cold and damp, and it was only towards the end of the month, 24–28 November, that the weather changed enough for additional training to take place. On Friday, 28th, John and Bob Edwards flew to Farnborough for tests in the decompression chamber, where Henry Roxburgh was conducting research on oxygen systems that made high-altitude flying possible. They then carried out a series of high-altitude exercises, which delighted them both. Records from the archive of the RAF Institute of Aviation Medicine show that Flying Officer Edwards and Pilot Officer McGhee (sic) completed tests to 38,000 feet and were 'considered suitable for high altitude flying'.

Writing about the tests only a day later, Sunday, 30 November, safely back at The Grange, John commented: 'I did the tests just fine but the best part is I now know a lot more about altitude and oxygen. I feel like Icarus but I shall be careful to protect my wings!' That experience and knowledge probably saved his life when a week later, in a practice high-altitude dogfight, he had forgotten to connect into his aircraft's oxygen supply and passed out at 22,000 feet. He came to in a high-speed dive just in time to pull out, much to the horror of Rod Smith and Jack Coleman, who were certain he had totally lost control – in their words 'lost it'.

That night in the bar of The Grange, after several pints of locally brewed ale had been consumed, there was a banter between all the officers about daring and fear. 'You just have to be mad enough' was Jack's response – looking at John, who did not respond immediately. He seemed to stop and consider his reply: 'If you don't have faith you can't take the risk,' he said. 'I think I've been testing it out all my life.' They all laughed together and passed round more drinks. Outside the icy wind was cutting, and Rod reminded them all how lucky they were to be alive and warm. 'Think of those poor beggars across the road sleeping in tents.'

Conversation turned to memories. It began with thoughts about Kit, and then, as if to lighten the mood, John reminded them how Kit had led them all out into the freezing darkness only weeks before, 'and we followed,' said John – 'and it was all your fault,' he added with a sweeping gesture to the group. 'If you hadn't come in and told us all about that sheep, we'd never have got so filthy and frozen.' Rod joked that none of them had got as muddy as him. 'I was all for giving up trying to get it – if you hadn't pretended to be its brother and bleat at it, it would have given up on me.'

'That's just it.' said John. 'If you hadn't dared to reach out to get it and we hadn't all hung onto you, it would have died by morning stuck there in the mud. Hey, we just saved it, and when we'd got it out, and it shook itself, bleated and hobbled off into the dark, we cheered – that was a good feeling.' 'Ten Canadian Officers save a sheep,' said Jack. 'I can see Hart's report now.' They all roared with laughter.

Chapter 12

December Dawns

On 1 December 1941, a Monday, the pilots of 'A' and 'B' Flight assembled to be told whether the weather would be suitable for flying. Fortunately, a wind had picked up overnight from the south-west, which moved the low grey cloud to reveal a bright blue beyond. Splitting the timing for take-off, 'A' Flight left for convoy patrols over the North Sea from 9.30 a.m. and John was one of the first to leave in his enthusiasm to be airborne. The Operations Record Book for that day shows 30 air-crew and almost 200 ground crew operational.

Squadron Leader Morrison had led one of the morning sorties, and on his return to base at 13.10 he met up with John, who was sitting out-side the dispersal hut. Because the cloud had lifted, the sun shone warmly, and, making the most of the weather, the two men decided to walk back to the Mess at The Grange. They took the short cut, not following the road, but going through the woods towards the Hall, which was poised in the sunlight on the cliff edge overlooking the Trent Valley. As they came to a clearing near the edge of the tall trees, John stopped and, grasping Morrison's arm, gestured to look upwards. They stood in silence, watch-ing. High against the unbroken blue were huge circling birds cruising on the air. They slowly and seemingly effortlessly floated in circles adjusting their direction. Not wanting to disturb the moment, Jack lowered his voice. 'What are they?' he asked in apparent disbelief. 'Buzzards,' replied John, as their familiar cry called across the silence.

The two men stood and watched their effortless cruising until they were, within minutes, distant specks. 'That's amazing,' said Jack, 'I didn't know.'

John interrupted. 'They live on this ridge. I've watched them for weeks on days like today. They like fine weather, like us, and they're using the thermals here to climb and soar upwards as if for ever. I always take this short cut through the woods on days like today, just hoping I'll see them flying. When I'm up there I think of them and how inspiring flying really is.'

As they moved off, Jack paused and commented: 'If you hadn't stopped, I'd have missed it. You're right, it's an amazing thing we do – I'll remember that for ever.'

The unexpected heat from the afternoon sun had the usual consequences on the landscape, and, as the sun lowered in the western sky, the cold damp rose and became fog. So the weather closed in again. Abbreviated terms generally used for describing mechanical problems now appeared in pilots' log books: 'Weather u/s. [unserviceable]'

It was not surprising that, when all flying was cancelled, attempts were made to keep pilots and aircrew meaningfully occupied. Lectures were a common feature on essential but uninspiring subjects such as flare paths. Jack Coleman took the opportunity provided by bad weather to drive over to see John, which in turn gave him the excuse to miss the flare path lecture in Wellingore Hall.

The two men spent about two hours in The Grange Mess, and after a few drinks walked across the road and through the Hall grounds to make their way towards the airfield. Jack hadn't been to the village or seen the Hall ever before, and he stopped to admire the size of the building.

'How many guys have we got in here?' he asked.

'About 200,' said John, 'and then about another 150 in these tents', as with a sweep of his arm he indicated the rows of tents pitched on the south side of the Hall.

'There's a lot of you here then.'

'Yes,' said John. 'Together with us in our Mess there's over 400.'

'What a place,' said Jack. 'How old is it? It can't be that old surely?'

John shrugged his shoulders. 'There's an inscription on the font dated 1750, but the locals say there was a bigger house here on this site earlier than that. They knocked that down to build this.'

'There's nothing as old as that back at home,' said Jack, surprised. 'Someone must have had a whole heap of dollars to build that.' They stood and looked out across the limestone escarpment, and could just make out two or three church towers, which identified distant villages.

'That's not all,' said John. 'The locals have found flint tools – evidence of this being inhabited thousands of years ago. Come on – and I'll show you something else.'

They followed a track down through the Hall grounds to a small lake, and then climbed a steeper bank up towards thickly planted and over-

grown woodland. Soon they came to a steeply raised bank overgrown
with shrubs and weeds.

'What do you make of that?' asked John laughing. Jack had no idea.

'Go on then,' he replied.

'Come and look at this,' said John, leading the way. He pushed back
bracken and stunted bushes to reveal an opening. 'Careful,' he warned
Jack, as he indicated a huge cavernous hole.

'What the hell is that for?' Jack questioned.

'I'll show you,' said John. 'Follow me – but take care.'

He turned round where he stood, got down on his knees, shuffled back-
wards and started to descend. As he disappeared, he gestured for Jack to
follow him. There was nothing to illuminate their slow descent on the
iron rungs fixed to the wall. Gradually their eyes became accustomed to
the darkness, and Jack could see they were descending into a huge brick-
built cavern.

'You OK?' asked John, as he reached the bottom, and, as Jack joined
him, he declared:, 'You're mad, you're always on to something different –
what is this place?'

Not far from where they were standing in the dim light, Jack could see
the outlines of a skeleton and John noticed him looking,

'I guess it's either a dog or a fox – poor devil it must have fallen in and
died. No one would have known it was here – they couldn't have got it out
anyway.'

They looked up the iron ladder to the shaft of light at the place they
had entered. It was like a tomb. John's voice echoed around the walls as
he nonchalantly intoned.

'Let us cease from pitying the dead, for after death there comes no
other calamity.'

'Who said that apart from you?' Jack asked, smiling.

'Palladas,' said John, 'I've used it before, at Rugby, when I wrote "Brave
New World".'

'I like it,' said Jack. 'You can write it on my tombstone – unless of course,
you go first!'

They looked at each other, smiling, and embraced in the damp graveyard space, neither sharing their inner fear that death could be so near
or so far away.

Once safely out of the cavern, Jack asked: 'What the hell was that built
for?'

John replied with modest authority: 'Oh it's an ice house, that's why it's near the lake. Long before ice boxes were invented, they just collected ice from the lake in winter, stored it in there, and that kept meat, fish and fruit fresh until it was needed up at the Hall. Is that not clever?'

Jack put his arm around him as they moved off together to walk to the airfield, commenting: 'You never cease to surprise me!'

'I don't need to,' said John. 'You're my best . . .' He wanted to say 'friend', but the last word would not come. He paused then finished the sentence with 'ever'. They both stood in silence and after a moment John quietly said: 'In the end, it's not the years in your life, it's the life in your years!'[58]

Chapter 13

Week Commencing 7 December 1941

The Operations Record Book (ORB) for 7 December records: 'Weather favourable for flying and a considerable amount of activity.' It was the busiest day for take-offs and landings since the squadron had been formed: '41 sorties were carried out' as well as aerobatics at 10,000 feet, convoy patrols, formation flying and practice scrambles.

No one in Lincolnshire could have been aware of the terrible air attacks that were taking place thousands of miles away at Pearl Harbor. The rehearsals in Lincolnshire seemed remote from the horror that brought America to declare war on Japan on 8 December 1941.

In Wellingore, 412 Squadron, unaware of these events, began practice with formation flying for pilots from both 'A' and 'B' Flights at different times in the day. Taking advantage of not being ordered to the first practice of the day, John sought out Hart Massey to fulfil a promise made days earlier over a drink to 'take him up for a spin'. Hart was eager to fly, and, although the weather was cloudy with occasional rain, blue sky was evident through chance breaks in the cloud. Much to John's delight, they drove together to the airfield in Hart's open-top MG sports car, and then quickly took off in a Magister. They soon broke through the low cloud, and for about half an hour toured the locality from about 1,500 feet. While they were airborne, an aircraft, a Spitfire Vb, flown by Sergeant Pilot McCrimmon, crashed on landing. Fortunately, the pilot escaped unharmed, but accidents never seemed far away.

Unable to fly himself, Hart was genuinely appreciative of his flight and on landing related the whole experience to aircrew outside the dispersal hut, as if they had little or no experience of flying themselves. While some pilots waited to take part in formation flying, others, who had already flown, joked that Hart 'ought to try a Spit'. He laughed at the suggestion, declaring that the cockpit was only built for the pilot, but then Rod Smith shouted across to the group, 'I'll squeeze him in.' The bets were on among the others pilots as to whether Rod would dare and whether Hart, as the Intelligence Officer, would take the risk!

By mid-afternoon, John was sitting outside the dispersal hut, together with a whole group of waiting aircrew from 'A' and 'B' Flights, to see if Rod would keep his promise. Towards late afternoon – at 4 p.m. to be precise – flight logs concur that Rod Smith took off from WCI for 'local flying'. What was not recorded was that, in the same Spitfire, Rod had a passenger – namely, Hart Massey.[59]

> I sat on my parachute but didn't have it on. Hart sat on my lap with his feet on the rear spar. I had my legs around Hart's, that's my left hand on the throttle and my right arm around Hart's waist and my hand on the control column. I had to change hands to raise and lower the under carriage, which caused a slight (but temporary) dip right after lift-off. We did pass a Lancaster over Lincoln and they certainly looked us over!![60]

Twenty minutes later they landed safely back at WCI and were greeted to a standing ovation. That night the Mess at the Hall was buzzing with the story, and eventually Hart, being so small, was lifted up on to a table, where he announced that to celebrate his first 'solo' flight he was 'getting them in for everyone'.

More than seventy men drank a toast to celebrate 'Hart's first flight'.[61] It is sometimes said that any excuse will do for a party, and the revelry was at its height when Hart pressed John's arm and, indicating with a move of his head that they should move towards the door, asked, 'Got a minute?' Then, in the semi-darkness of the hallway, he said to John: 'There's some bad news mate.' John stared at him but said nothing. Hart continued: 'It's Jack, he's been reported missing over France – he went down over the sea – they don't think there's . . .'

John just shook his head and finished the sentence, 'much chance'.

'Sorry,' said Hart, 'but I thought you should be the first to know, since he was your best mate . . .'

'Yeah, yeah,' said John, making for the doorway and out into the night.[62]

John Ronald Coleman, known as Jack, was 23 years and 5 months old when he died. He and John had often joked about whether June was a lucky month to be born, John's birth being on 9 June 1922 and Jack on

27 June 1918. As Jack was four years older than John, there had been an understanding between them that Jack would 'look out for John!' That agreement was now over.

On 8 December at 11.00 a.m. Spitfire aircraft had taken off from a forward airbase in the south of England to provide cover for bomber air-craft in a strike over enemy territory. Jack was piloting one of those Spit-fires and was shot down.

A detail in the official letter sent from the Air Ministry in London in mid-January 1942, which was sent to his sister Eileen as next of kin, simply said:

> At approximately 1135 a.m. a considerable number of enemy aircraft intercepted the squadron off the coast of France. In the combat which ensued one of our aircraft was seen to go down with smoke pouring from it, but as the pilot did not, or was unable to, advise his ident-ification, it is not known whether this was your brother, or another pilot who also failed to return to base. No further information has, however, been received either of your brother or of his aircraft.
> In the absence of any definite news of your brother, it will be nec-essary after the lapse of approximately 6 months from the date that he was reported missing to presume his death for official purposes. When such action is contemplated, a further letter will be addressed to you.

John just walked down the short drive from the Officers' Mess across the road and into the grounds of the Hall. He walked slowly, deliberately avoiding other people, and made his way through the tents in the garden and across the fields to the wood. Here he slowed down, almost careless in his direction, and eventually found himself at the ice house. He pushed his way through the bracken and undergrowth to the top of the mound that formed the roof. He stopped, and finding a large broken bole of rot-ting timber, sat down. So many conflicting ideas crossed his mind, and he so much needed to focus his thoughts – anger and anguish dominated his thinking but gradually words came from within to express the feeling, the frustration, the loss:

> Now I have heard the voices of the dead
> I have read out the writing on the wall
> And wearied out my brain upon the secret
> And torn my mind against the jagged dark

And still I find no answer to it all!
Then it seems that I am doomed to extinction
And all my loves and hates will die with me.
No force is left to save me from this waste,
This careful shaping of a life in vain,
Which must, before it lives, find time to die![63]

The fine line between life and death was a constant. To be killed in action against the enemy at least gave some cause or reason for dying, but nothing else. Accidental mistakes, which could have fatal consequences, were a constant worry. The very next day John was flying Interception missions during the day, and then, with Rod Smith and Doug Powell, he was out late practising night flying. They took off around 22.20 and within thirty minutes – disaster. Doug had crashed, smashing his aircraft to a wreck. Simultaneously, John was struggling to bring his aircraft in to land because of a malfunction with the air speed indicator.[64] Fortunately he was in radio contact with Rod, and, after flying a circuit in close formation, Rod led him in to land safely. One crisis seemed to follow another.

John's flying log simply recorded: 'Airspeed indicator U/S. Brought in in formation by P/O Smith.' It seemed that, because all of them were pushing the boundaries of their flying experience, more accidents were possible, even likely.

The tensions created by these kinds of experiences, on a daily basis, were very stressful. Even young men who appeared to have a carefree attitude to it all could easily become irritable and aggressive when off duty. Senior and more experienced officers were on constant alert for the younger men to ensure some kind of balance in the daily routines of their lives.

December was not a comfortable month for men with time to spare. Fog, drizzle, low grey cloud or icy wind determined the pattern for each day, and, with the end of the year approaching, there were plans for Christmas parties. Many men who had crossed the Atlantic would make their celebrations in Wellingore, but John planned to go south and meet up with Elinor at Rugby and join her family for the festive season. Writing to Dermott, he enquired when they could meet soon, adding: 'But I cannot be certain of dates until I know when I can be with Elinor – she is always in my thoughts, and I want to make the most of whatever leave I can get to be with her.'[65]

He was willingly distracted from reflecting on what might be when, on

10 December, there were aircraft that needed air testing, and he was, as always, a ready volunteer. Most of that afternoon he was in his element, testing his responses and skills to control different machines. He loved being at the centre of purposeful activities and relished the banter between himself and the ground crew about the handling characteristics of various aircraft.

Chapter 14

Disaster in the Air

The morning of 11 December dawned as another grey and bitterly cold day. There was no reason to leave the warmth of the Mess at The Grange, except that instructions had been posted for formation flying, and twenty or more pilots made their different ways to the airfield. The dispersal hut was soon full of men, changing clothing, joking, smoking. The metal pot-bellied stove had been well stoked, and the fire gave a background comfort. By about 10.30 a succession of Spitfires was ready for their respective pilots from 'A' and 'B' Flights. The cloud base was low over the airfield, about 1,500 feet, but the breaks in the cloud layer revealed a bright blue sky beyond. The Spitfires followed standard take-off routines, heading in a northerly direction to take part in a wing formation practice with a Lincolnshire RAF squadron from Kirton Lindsey.

Almost immediately one aircraft, piloted by Rod Smith, left the line of ascending aircraft, a stream of white vapour pouring from the engine cowling near the propeller. Rod recalled: 'I realized at once that my engine coolant filler cap had not been fastened down and I left the squadron before it entered the cloud base and landed quickly. It only took a moment to have the cap fastened, but it was then too late to go looking for the squadron.'[66]

Once above the cloud layer, the aircraft came into formation, and John, being in 'A' Flight, was wing man to Squadron Leader Kit Morrison. The exercise went well in an almost clear sky, and after an hour Jack Morrison, as leader, decided that they would return to base. The aircraft were in a close formation as they descended rapidly through the cloud base. Morrison, followed by John, followed by Sergeant Pilot Dwayne Linton, followed by Pilot Officers Gartshore and Ellis.

The noise of impact of one object on another is often closely associated with the materials that are in collision. But nothing, no words ever, could describe the searing, tearing explosion as the Spitfire flown by John collided with an Oxford trainer flying just below the cloud base. Out of control, both disintegrating aircraft plunged earthwards and in seconds both pilots were instantly killed on impact with the ground.

This is Rod Smith's account of what had happened:

> When the wing formation practice ended the wing leader told
> Jack to take the squadron home. Jack returned with the squadron
> to within a few miles of Wellingore. They were still above the cloud
> layer when Jack noticed a small hole going right down through it.
> As was normal in those days, he preferred to lead the squadron
> down a hole rather than do a slower and more stately let-down in
> the cloud. When sweeps or exercises were over, squadrons often had
> only five or six minutes of fuel left and were anxious to get their
> wheels on the ground. So Jack ordered the squadron into line astern
> behind him and dived down through the hole almost vertically.
> The others formed one long line behind him about 100 yards apart,
> each following the aircraft in front. Their speed built up to about
> 450 mph. The controls become very heavy at that speed. Only the
> elevators remain sensitive, the Spitfire being absolutely remarkable
> for its ability to pull out of a fast steep dive quickly. Unfortunately
> the hole happened to be in Cranwell's northerly circuit and the
> Oxford happened to pass under the bottom of the hole as the
> squadron was coming out of it. Spitfires cruise at more than 4 miles
> a minute, the distance between Wellingore and Cranwell. When they
> dive at 450 mph, they are moving at 650 feet a second. It is little
> wonder the Oxford, moving at slow circuit speed, was not avoided,
> once it had the misfortune to cross the path of eleven diving Spitfires.

Moments later the ragged formation of Spitfires approached Wellingore airfield from the south at about 1,000 feet. They made a circuit of the airfield before coming in to land. As the first aircraft touched down, the operations telephone rang to say that a Spitfire had crashed between Wellingore and Cranwell. Rod Smith was watching the squadron land and, being told of the telephone message, took off immediately.

> I took off before the rest of the squadron had landed, and as I

turned towards Cranwell I quickly spotted a crashed Spitfire burning
in a farmer's field, near a wood, a mile or so north of Cranwell. One
of its wings was partly upside down in the wreckage, showing its
underside roundel and its classic elliptical fin. It looked like a broken,
beautiful bird.

The Royal Air Force Report Form 551 on Accidental Death dated 14 December 1941 states in Section 3: 'Description of injuries. Fractured cervical
and lumbar vertebrae. Multiple fractures of ribs.' Another Air Ministry
Technical Report of the same date states:

> The aircraft was inspected and it was found that the engine had
> become detached from the airframe, being found 400 yards away.
> The airframe was completely wrecked and burnt. The port wing
> was found 700 yards away from the airframe, the wing tip being a
> further 300 yards away.

Police Sergeant H. Challand was on duty in his substation office on the
outskirts of the small market town of Sleaford when a call came for him
to attend an accident in the vicinity of a group of buildings clustered
around Roxholm Hall. He knew the general direction from his substation and, with the time getting towards midday, he set off on his
bicycle to locate the incident. His notebook records that the weather con-
ditions were poor and he had to pedal hard against a penetrating cold
wind and freezing drizzle, which swept in from the south-west.

Some days later, called before a magistrate and three senior-ranking
Air Force officials at the main police station in Sleaford, Sergeant Challand
appeared unconcerned by the formality of the occasion when asked to
give his account of what he had seen. He had attended too many such
post-mortems recently and calmly stood to attention and slowly and
methodically opened his notebook, cleared his throat and began.

> Sir, on the morning of Friday 11th of December I was directed to
> leave my sub office to attend an accident approximately 4 miles
> away near a local landmark called Roxholm Hall. I arrived, sir, at
> the place at approximately 12:30 hours. As I approached I could see
> smoke rising from what appeared to be a small fire. As I got nearer
> I could see several men throwing buckets of water on the fire,
> collected from a small pond adjacent to where part of an aircraft

had clearly crashed. I quickly ascertained that the pilot was still trapped in what remained of the aircraft and as soon as it was safe to do so we wrenched back the canopy of the cockpit only to realize our worst fears: the pilot was dead. I followed the usual procedures and was assisted by a civilian, whom I later learned was the occupant of a small cottage adjacent to a nearby searchlight battery. Together we agreed that the pilot, a young man, was indeed dead, and nothing could be done to save him. The men who had been attending to the fire eventually succeeded in extinguishing the flames and there was nothing further that could be done.

As we stood and talked, I observed a Spitfire aircraft circling low overhead, as if examining the area around us. We discussed the cause of the crash and, not being a military man, I noted that some of the group commented that parts of the aircraft seemed to be missing and were not to be found in the immediate vicinity. The pilot had clearly not had any chance of escaping from a disintegrating aircraft.

As the Spitfire circled yet again above us my attention was attracted by another man running towards us shouting. He was gesticulating and directed my attention to another crashed aircraft across the fields from where we were standing. I immediately followed him as quickly as possible and in the distance I could make out an ambulance in a field. The ground was very wet from recent rain and our progress was slow, but as we got nearer I could see a group of people clustered together near the ambulance. I estimate there were six or seven men and a young girl who stood some way off from the group. She was restrained from getting closer to the group by a man who repeatedly shouted at her whom I took to be her father. His behaviour was in marked contrast to the motionless composure of the rest of the group of men.

As I got closer, two men, whom I took to be the ambulance driver and his assistant, were carefully lifting a stretcher into the vehicle on which there was obviously a body covered by a blanket. There was no sense of urgency in their actions and as the stretcher was slowly lowered into the back of the ambulance I concluded that this pilot must also be dead.

The group of men remained silent, and one of them directed my attention by pointing to the ground to his right. I moved towards the place and saw a deep scooped hollow. It was a dark hollow and at its deepest point a pool of what I took to be blood had stained the loam black. I knew for certain that if a man's body had made that indentation on the earth and then lost that much blood then he was certainly dead sir. Yes sir, dead!

His voice wavered momentarily.

He was certainly dead.

As the ambulance engine started up, the group clustered closer together, including the young girl. In silence they watched as it slowly retraced the path of its earlier tyre tracks across the rutted beet field. It reached the road, turned south, picked up speed and was quickly gone, leaving the onlookers saddened and speechless. The young girl now clung to her father, sobbing.

Having witnessed the pilot separated from his plane fall from the sky without being able to deploy his parachute, the young lady was very distraught, Sir, and she just kept repeating the same phrase, 'Him never 'ad a chance, him never 'ad a chance.'

Her cries of despair drifted on the icy wind, as, together with the older man, she slowly trudged towards a nearby roadside cottage.

Meanwhile, Rod had quickly landed his Spitfire back at Wellingore and later remembered what then happened.

On landing I was told that John had not come back with the squadron. Hart and I and the other deputy flight commander got into Hart's car and drove down a road lying just east of Wellingore and leading in the direction of Cranwell. We soon found the crash, a little bit off to the west of the road. We also saw an ambulance heading away from us and down the road towards Cranwell. We parked the car and walked across the field up to within about 70 feet from the crash. We did not come closer because some of the cannon ammunition was exploding in the fire.

    We stood alongside another group of people – we all seemed rooted to the spot, the place where death had come so suddenly from the sky.

The cloud ceiling had begun to clear and patches of sunshine were showing here and there. As we were leaving we noticed a hole in the ground about 200 feet east of the crash. We walked over to it and saw that it was the imprint of John's body, stamped so severely in the soft soil; it was as deep as a man's arm. The impact of man on earth must have been tremendous. He had struck the ground with his back. Nothing remained there except a large pool of blood in the bottom of the hole. We then briefly walked over to the wreckage of the Oxford, about a third of a mile to the south-east. The desire to fill in or hide this terrible hollow seemed the only way to address the horror of it. We returned sadly to Wellingore.

Ruth Love was the young woman at the crash scene. At the time of the accident she lived with her parents, in a cottage that still stands today by the roadside. She witnessed the crash less than a mile from her front door.

On 12 and 16 December the Lincolnshire Deputy Coroner Hubert Pym held an inquest in the sick quarters at RAF College, Cranwell, and returned a verdict of accidental death on LAC Griffin. He released his body for cremation at Oxford Crematorium, where his name is recorded with others killed on active service.

No one at the scene of this terrible event would have known that on the very same day that John gave his life in the service of his country, President Roosevelt declared war on Germany: 11 December 1941 was a day that the world would remember for ever.

Chapter 15

Preparation for the funeral

There were twenty or so pilots who assembled to listen to Jack Morrison. The liberal amount of alcohol that had been consumed had lifted morale and created an accommodating atmosphere for the Squadron Leader to address a difficult matter. His explanation was sympathetic but informed, generous but objective, as he outlined how routines had to be followed to the letter in order to minimize the chance of such errors of judgement ever happening again.

After telephone discussions with the flying training section at RAF Cranwell, it was determined that a no-fly zone needed to be created around the college to protect trainee pilots from another fatal occurrence. There were murmurs of agreement, and, as Morrison finished with his intentions for future flight plans, it was almost with relief that he concluded: 'Remember, this must never happen again.' Many officers wanted to think beyond the next few days and discuss what opportunities and threats lay ahead, but it was Hart Massey's arrival that changed the direction of the discussions. Not being a pilot, he had not been part of the earlier meeting – but as Intelligence Officer he had been delegated to bring to the Mess the orders for the funeral service, the outline of which he had written on a single sheet of paper. Questions were raised immediately about who would carry the coffin, and not surprisingly many officers offered, indeed demanded, that they should be chosen.

The discussion became quite lively, with some of the officers suggesting their friends rather than themselves – everyone agreed that Rod and Bob should be two of the bearer party, but Hart wanted to join them. Hart's orders from Flying Officer Howe, who was acting on behalf of his Digby station commander, determined that there should be a bearer party of twelve men under the charge of Sergeant Graham. Hart wanted to be included, but suddenly a spirited argument began, disputing whether

Hart should or should not be one of the officers who carried the coffin. The discussion became quite heated, when suddenly Pilot Officer Young started to laugh.

'You wouldn't do it, Hart,' he said, 'it would be all over the place.'

'What would?' asked Hart indignantly.

'The coffin man – the coffin – you're too short, stand you in line next to Rod or Ellis – they're six foot and more and look at you.'

Hart was furious with Young – disagreed and tried to put his point of view again – tempers began to be raised as others joined in – Hart couldn't or just wouldn't agree.

Rod came to the rescue – under the window there was a wooden bench six or seven feet in length. He lifted it up and carried it to the centre of the room.

'Come on Ellis,' he directed, 'you get that end', and he ordered Gartshore and Davidson to put down their drinks and join in. Young and Davis added to the group and, standing three in a line, in two rows, they positioned the bench on their shoulders.

'Now do you see it Hart?' asked Rod. 'We're going to be holding it above your head, got it?'

Hart sighed – looked downcast. 'I only wanted to do my bit for Maggie,' he said.

Ellis put his hand on Hart's shoulder. 'Tell you what, Hart, you carry the wreath for all of us – how about that – lead the way?'

Hart moved between the lines and stood at the front proudly.

'Yes, that'll be fine, I can do that, I don't feel left out now.'

'You're not left out,' said Rod. 'We're all doing this together for our best mate Maggie, let's drink to it!' And they did.

Chapter 16

Funeral

As dawn broke, Saturday, 13 December, appeared to be another grey overcast day with an icy chill in the wind. Snow showers were forecast in other counties, but as the funeral party prepared to leave Wellingore flurries of snow drifted in. The funeral of John Magee was scheduled for 1430 hours. Officers left The Grange and assembled in the grounds of Wellingore Hall, where the escort and bearer parties joined them at 1245 hours. Transport had been organized, and a succession of military vehicles drew up to convey all those attending the funeral at a village named Scopwick, close to 412's main base at Digby. Meanwhile, representatives from 609 and 92 Squadrons from Digby, which included personnel of the firing party and trumpeters, were assembling at the main Guard Room for 1330 hours.

All the groups met up at the crossroads at Scopwick at 1415 hours, and the tender carrying the coffin left the mortuary at the Digby Station Sick Quarters at 1400 hours.

The officer in charge of the funeral party was Squadron Leader Jack Morrison, with an escort party led by Flight Lieutenant Archer, Sergeant Backhouse and thirty other men detailed by 412 Squadron. The bearer party was coordinated by Sergeant Graham and included twelve men: P/O Ellis, P/O Young, Sgt Brookhouse, A/C Calvert, A/C Strowgler, A/C Brown, A/C Gammon, 023 Davis, 155 Coombes, P/O Davidson, P/O Gartshore and P/O Smith.

The military graveyard at Scopwick had been created on the edge of the village and was surrounded on three sides by agricultural land. Over a number of years it had been the place of rest for many men who had been killed in action.

The graveside service was led by the Digby padre, a Canadian, Squadron Leader F. K. Burton, assisted by Reverend Lewis E. Barker, vicar of

Scopwick. The assembled men and women who had come to pay their last respects to John filled the graveyard. Some men, particularly those who had been chosen to carry the coffin, were clearly moved by the solemnity of the occasion, and each pondered his own thought on losing such a dear friend. The members of this closely knit community, who worked together day by day and depended so much on each other in carrying out their duties, were horrified and numbed by any misfortune to their own – but the death of a friend and colleague left such an empty void.

They were called to attention, and as the trumpeters' lamenting call cried out over the Lincolnshire landscape, flurries of snow drifted in from a sky breaking as if to a new dawn. John Magee was laid to rest.

The service concluded, some men left in military order, while others stood in silence. Jack Morrison, with his duties completed, walked slowly across to a group of his own sergeants and pilots clustered near the gateway. They were downcast, disconsolate and uncertain of the words best suited to the moment. Jack turned to Rod and asked: 'What should we say Rod – what would he have said?'

Rod paused. 'I suppose,' he began, 'since we're on the edge of this field, we ought to remember his favourite poet and what he once wrote.'

'Go on,' said Jack, 'tell us.'

Rod paused and gathered himself. Slowly and deliberately he quoted Rupert Brooke's words:

> If I should die, think only this of me
> That there's some corner of a foreign field
> That is forever England. . . .

There were no other words. Hands were clasped, smiles fought back the tears, and they left to go back to flying.

Chapter 17

Back at The Grange

The small upstairs bedroom at The Grange had been a welcome refuge for the officers who shared the house as a Mess. The rooms on the ground floor were meeting places and what had been a lounge and dining room became a bar and command area. Back at their Mess, they reflected on the discomfort of the afternoon over drinks, and it was not long before a toast was proposed in the usual tradition and the drinks were allocated to John's Mess bill. Upstairs, Bob Edwards slumped on the bed in the room he had shared with John: he was lonely, depressed and just waiting. Jack Morrison had told him that Pilot Officer Young would be moving in with him, and all John's possessions needed moving immediately. There was only one person who could handle the reorganization, and that was the batman they had both shared – Jim Hartland. A knock on the door announced his arrival. Bob didn't move but shouted 'Yeah'. 'I believe you wanted me sir,' began Jim Hartland. 'Yeah, yeah, that's right,' Bob replied. 'Just clear this bloody lot out. Pilot Officer Young is sleeping in here tonight,' he said, pointing to John's bed. 'But sir,' began Jim. Bob interrupted, shouting, 'Look Hartland, I just can't stand it, it's bad enough him not being here – just get it all out of my sight – and be quick about it.' 'Yes sir,' came the reply, and Jim smartly left the room, only grimacing when he was well down the corridor and out of site. He was surprised by the outburst, but familiar with the kind of tensions that were created when any accident occurred.

He soon returned with an assortment of boxes he had taken from the downstairs pantry. Bob hadn't moved from the bed. 'When I've packed it in these,' he asked, referring to the boxes, 'what shall I do with it?'

'For God's sake, do what you bloody well like – just get it out of my sight and quick. I can't cope with it all around me.'

Bob and John had shared this back bedroom for almost three months.

They had slept less than an arm's length apart on iron-framed single beds and had shared everything.

The room was cluttered. Boots filled the hearth of the unused fireplace, and the mantelpiece was heaped with shaving gear, photos, overfilled ashtrays and empty cups and glasses. Trousers and shirts hung on hooks knocked into the picture rail; heavy leather flying kit hung drying from the sagging curtain pole. Boxes spewed their contents under both beds, and the cupboard with only one remaining door was overflowing.

Hartland had managed to keep some sense of purpose in this chaos where the two men had tipped the contents of their lives. He had regularly sorted out dirty socks, shirts and underwear for washing, scraped mud from boots before polishing them and cleaned down uniforms to create some semblance of order. Nothing had been too much trouble for him, and he admired and at times revered their shared passion of purpose, exhilaration with flying. As he stuffed John's possessions into an already over-full old leather suitcase, he mused on how out of character it was for his officer, Bob Edwards, to behave in this unexpected way. He was very upset.

As he attempted to buckle down the bulging suitcase, odd bits of clothing hung out on all sides. Undeterred he stood on the lid and quickly braced the leather together with a large strap and buckle. Next he pulled papers, notebooks and letters from a brown stained pot cupboard they had shared between the two beds. Bob sorted out his own belongings, and Hartland dumped all the rest into another battered cardboard box.

Neither spoke, but Bob's actions were becoming noticeably frantic. Having said he couldn't bring himself to touch anything of John's, he now swept anything that was not his into a second cardboard box with no sense of order or care. It was as if, by removing everything that had belonged to John from his immediate vision, he would ease the pain of losing him.

Hartland methodically and silently continued; hairbrush, tobacco and pipe, two scarves, notebooks, pens and pencils, a bundle of letters, several books, leather gauntlets and a flying helmet. As they seemed to come to the end of the collecting, Bob just barked at Hartland, 'OK you finish it now' and stormed out.

Jim sighed and sat on John's bed, surrounded by the boxes of John's belongings. He paused to gather himself before carrying them downstairs. As he reflected on the whole sorry affair he noticed a small folded piece of paper protruding from under the pillow. He picked it up and saw the word 'Johnny' scrawled across it. He didn't recognize the writing and cautiously opened it, feeling a sense of both curiosity and guilt.

It was short and to the point. He smiled to himself as he recognized the author from the signature – the attractive brunette who helped prepare meals for officers in the downstairs kitchens. It simply read: 'Thanks for a real night out at the Bear Pit, see you tonight when my shift ends. Louise xx.'

He mused over the end of the message and wondered how she would cope with not having Johnny around. They had been 'going out' for about two weeks. He sighed, got up from the bed and purposefully tossed all John's remaining effects on to the blanket on the bed. He took a short length of wire from his pocket and grabbing each corner of the blanket bound them tightly together. As he lifted the improvised sack to take it away, Bob returned.

'That's it, Sir. Thank you, Sir.' Bob didn't reply.

Many years after the war was over, Jim Hartland recalled his time at Wellingore and his recollections of John.

> I joined the RAF at the age of 19 early in 1940. I was only 5' 4" in height so there were lots of things I wasn't allowed to do. Eventually I became a batman. Orderlies and batmen were trades in the RAF. I was driven to The Grange at Wellingore late one night as I recall, with my instructions to find the officers' quarters in the morning. There I would be told my duties. In the meantime it was tumbling down with rain. A number of tents were at the back of the large old hall, as I will call it. I had got to get into one of these for the night. After trying one or two flaps that were fastened, an English voice cried out, 'Get in here mate.' Squelching through the mud, I finally got down onto a mattress lying there for a grateful body. I never saw that airman before moving the next day. The other ranks, as I will call them, ate up in one of the old hall rooms. We queued in a line to get breakfast at an improvised counter and sat down at small tables. The cookhouse staff were Canadians. I also remember all the old rooms in The Grange were all used up for some type of work. There did seem to be so many people about.
>
> The then eight, nine or ten officers, mostly pilots, had to be domestically looked after. I was taken (upstairs and downstairs), briefly told who to look after and in as many words get on with it as a 'batman', cleaning shoes, sewing buttons on, making beds, taking

laundry, pressing suits, serving meals, serving drinks at night, polishing glasses, polishing furniture, in other words making sure the squadron pilots were looked after in the true traditions of a batman.

The first time I met P/O J. Magee I thought to myself what a sissy, what have they given me now. I called him Longfellow Magee, so did the other members of the staff. But as time wore on he changed. The R.C.A.F. made a man out of him and, if it comes to that, so did England. I could never do anything for him unless he said 'You need not have bothered', 'It was okay', 'What do you rush for, have a rest, take it easy!', 'What you panicking for.' I was not allowed to call him sir, and, believe me, that was one of the main things that got me to like J. Magee. At times he had a nasty habit of throwing his things about, very hard to wake up, boy shake him. I used to call him all things behind his back, but still we got on well, in fact very well. I'll tell you another thing: I could talk to him as though I was talking to my own pal.

The men of 412 liked him, sir, as much as I did: his ways, his manner, his work, and his cooperation with the men. He was a grand flyer, crazy on flying, plenty of guts and believe me, sir, he lived up to his nationality. I am sure that he died the way he wanted to (flying).

If an accident had happened, or a pilot was missing, etc., no words were spoken. But an eerie silence remained in The Grange for days and even to this day I can remember how it kept coming into my head that guys like him just didn't deserve to die! He joined up two different skills, flying and poetry, like no one had done before. It seemed like he was supposed, I think the proper word is destined, to leave his words to help us understand our creator, for ever.

Chapter 18

Hugh and Elinor at Rugby

Breakfast at Rugby was an early morning ritual for Hugh Lyon and his family. They always sat down together in the dining room of School House. Hugh often reminded friends and family that it was the best meal of the day. Because of food rationing, there were several of the masters who welcomed the invitation to a working breakfast. Sometimes these started very early, lasting up to one and a half hours, but they always finished well before morning lessons began.

Tuesday, 16 December, was no different at its start from any other morning breakfast. When the family were on their own, Hugh would read *The Times* newspaper, but never when there were visitors or other masters.

As he enjoyed a bowl of porridge, conversation around the table enquired about how much vacation studying Elinor needed to do, and, as the conversation developed, Hugh was distracted by the newspaper, which was partly opened next to him. He picked it up and opened it the better to study it. The chatter round the table continued.

Suddenly he quickly got up, dropped the newspaper on the table, wiped his mouth with his serviette and rushed out. Nan and Barbara called after him, 'What's the matter Daddy?' 'Is everything all right dear?' There was no reply.

Surprised at Hugh's sudden departure, everyone in the room fell silent. Then Elinor slowly got up and walked over to where the newspaper lay open on the table.

Recalling that moment many years later she said: 'Something just told me – it was the way father left the room – I just knew it was bad – I don't think I thought 'it's John', but there it was. I just stood there looking at the black ink until it all went blurred and then I just rushed outside!'

Outside she ran – then walked, the tears coming, accompanied by a strange coughing and spluttering as if she was going to be sick.

'I walked and ran in bursts on and on, going nowhere until I came to the Tosh – I just found an unlocked door into one of the changing rooms and sat on a bench and sobbed my heart out!'

Nan and Barbara knew better than to chase after Elinor. They too guessed what might be the cause of all the commotion. Having read the same announcement in the newspaper, Nan just held Barbara to her, with tears running down her face, as she slowly said: 'Our John – our John – he's gone – I don't believe it.'

Meanwhile, Elinor, in the chill damp sheds that were changing rooms, held her left hand, palm upwards, in her right hand. She was staring at and examining her left index finger. 'He never did tell me,' she sobbed. 'He promised he would tell me about that round scar on his first finger, this Christmas – I can't ask him now so I'll never know!'

In late January, when Elinor was back at Oxford, she had time on her own to reflect and think about John. She wrote the following poem.

J.G.M.
Remember now, how once we walked
In twilight clear and still
And filled our hearts with young delight
Last year, on Bredon Hill.

Those summer days, what brief bright hours
Brief joys, they had to bring
How sweet the summer had to be
For one who saw no spring.

Soon darkness comes to all things dear
Night falls on Bredon Hill.
But bright on your eternal fields
The sun is shining still.

Elinor recalled how she and John spent happy hours walking alone on Bredon Hill. Bredon Hill is in the county of Worcestershire, England, in the Vale of Evesham. Elinor copied the poem into the back of 'Poems by John Magee',[69] which he had sent her from Avon Old Farms School. It was never published in her lifetime, but she shared it with the author, with an agreement that it could be published 'if you think it's good enough'.

In July 1946 Hugh Lyon arranged a special service in the Chapel to celebrate the conclusion of hostilities and 'expressing thankfulness for victory'. It was a significant occasion, and there was standing room only at the back of the Chapel. The emotion Hugh felt for the occasion he conveyed in his first sentence.

> My friends. I have waited for this day for nearly seven years and now that it has come – my heart is very full.

The sentiments he then expressed were for all the pupils who had given their lives in the service of their country. John Magee could never have been far from his thoughts when he said:

> I am glad to see you here, I am only sorry that we could not have more of those who badly wished to come. But this peace which you have brought to us is still an uneasy peace, and there are Old Rugbeians on service all over the world.
>
> But, at a time like this, the thoughts of us all, I think, turn first to those who are not here for a more compelling reason still: those who, with you, faced the hazards of the past years, and paid the utmost price in fighting for their country and the freedom of the world. We are not (sic) for them but for ourselves, and for those who mourn them. We are proud of them, and we know that, in the years to come, their short and splendid lives will shine out as examples to all who follow. I often think of that (sic) – the loveliest perhaps of Brooke's sonnets – which ends:

> There are waters blown by changing winds to laughter
> And lit by the rich skies, all day. And after,
> Frost, with a gesture, stays the waves that dance
> And wandering loveliness. He leaves a white
> Unbroken glory, a gathered radiance,
> A width, a shining peace, under the night.

Chapter 19

Wellingore, the Woodsheds (1990)

Today, the casual visitor to the village of Wellingore would be unaware of the history that lies hidden behind many of its buildings. One such house lies at the centre, where it assertively fronts up to the roadside. This imposing property proclaims its Georgian origins and in autumn displays a garland of magenta ivy.

It is surprising, then, to find that this house conceals what was once the wood yard. For more than 100 years a straggle of large sheds, constructed in the tradition of the cliff villages in limestone with red pantile roofs, had been the focus of much of the estate management for the lords of the manor. For centuries they had occupied the nearby large Hall on the top of rising ground at the edge of the village and overlooking the Trent Valley.

The Hall was the family seat for the Nevilles, who historically were rich landowners. For several hundred years they had employed most of the residents of the village, either labouring on the land or caring for their Hall and maintaining the quality of life of its occupants. The innovation of the family knew no bounds, and in the nineteenth century they had put their ingenuity, creativity and wealth to good use by generating their own electricity. So, when darkness fell, while the rest of the inhabitants of the village lit their oil lamps and candles, the residents of the Hall basked in electric light and so became one of the first houses in the country to have a constant supply of electricity.

To achieve this, at some time in the past the woodsheds had been converted to house huge storage batteries, as tall as a man, and these in turn were charged by four huge generators. The electricity so supplied was conveyed underground through cables as thick as a man's arm to the Hall, which was more than half a mile distant. The reasoning for this seemingly inconvenient arrangement was quite simple. Every morning the huge fly wheels, which had been rested overnight, had to be hand cranked and fired with a cartridge. The noise and vibration were deafening, as the four engines revived the batteries from dawn for the remainder of the day. Consequently the generators and batteries were placed as far away as possible from the residents of the Hall, in order not to disturb their enjoyment of this unique luxury, electricity.

With the arrival of a national grid for the ready supply of electricity to everyone in the village, the sheds were no longer needed and so were returned to their earlier use. They were now once again the centre for the management of all the timber and the products derived from it for the hundreds of acres of the estate.

Barry Newstead was one of a number of men who daily maintained the routines of this busy yard. He was a short, thick-set and muscular man whose weather-beaten features disguised his 26 years of age. His boss and now owner of the yard was Chris Jefferies, whose father had been the estate foreman and had bought the house and yard from the Neville estate. The daily routine labour of lifting and shifting massive trunks of wood was the accepted task, and Chris had put Barry in charge of the yard, to set and maintain a vigorous routine that only a young man of his strength and stamina could sustain.

The roofs of the old stone buildings sagged with the weight of their history. The huge trees from landlord Neville's estate had been brought to this reinstated saw pit for the last fifty years, and it had once again become one of the many sources of income that had created the family wealth. Barry had served his apprenticeship like many before him in the depths of that saw pit, known as the grave, continually choking with reeking sawdust that stifled your breathing, chafed and irritated your skin and secreted itself in every crevice of your body and clothing.

Having served his years of apprenticeship in the grave, he was relieved that the technology had changed with the coming of electrical power. The main difference today for Barry was that, as he hauled on the tackle chains to lift the next massive trunk into position, he knew he would be directing the trunks straight to the mechanical saw, rather than hearing the cursing of the newest apprentice from the grave as the trunk was moved into position. Modern technology had taken the torturous physical demand from the work, and now a large and powerful electric motor was joined to the saw table by a whining and thrashing rotating belt, which drove the saw blade at a terrifying speed, showering the whole shed with splinters of wood.

Under stress, the engine noise increased as if in temper. To the trained ear it was always a warning sign of the strain on the action of the saw blade cutting the timber. If suddenly it backfired, the engine would jolt and throw off the drive belt with a snap like a whiplash that would sever a man's arm.

Familiar with these tantrums, Barry frequently anticipated what was about to happen and would dive to kill the engine. As it hissed to a halt he was joined by Chris, smiling.

'Have a break?' he questioned.

Barry nodded agreement as the din subsided, and they headed off to a roughly partitioned corner of the shed that served as a refuge and office. The kettle quickly screamed itself to boiling point, and two large beakers were filled with tea. As they perched on the rough planks that served as seats, Chris tugged a newspaper from his inside jacket pocket.

'Did yer see this?' he asked, pointing to a headline.

Barry, who never bought a newspaper and rarely tried to read one, shrugged and noisily sucked at his tea.

'It's about those Yankee astronauts and that rocket.'

'Yeah it's bloody terrible, there was nothing they could do – not a chance,' Barry retorted.

In the silence that followed they both just stared at the wall, imagining; then Chris just turned over the pages one after another that recounted the grief and disbelief of the American people. There really was nothing that could be said: the horror of it was all so far removed from these rain-soaked days in this remote Lincolnshire agricultural landscape.

Suddenly Chris stopped, and muttered.

'What y'r say?' asked Barry.

'It can't be,' said Chris. 'No, I just don't believe it, no, that can't be right.' There was a pause, Barry leant towards him.

'What the hell ay'r goin' on about?' he quizzed.

'It's this writing, these words,' said Chris, 'I've read it before. No, I've seen it before – y'r know, you remember, that young bloke who hung around here a lot on his time off, used to read to us, remember?'

'I don't know what the hell y'r on about.'

'You do,' Chris interrupted. 'Him that had that posh accent and was a Yank and used to hang around here, always askin' about the trees and wood and all that and tellin' us stuff about birds and planes divin' through the sky like eagles.'

Barry still looked uncertain but affirmed he could remember and murmured, 'Yeah, yeah.'

Slowly he straightened his shoulders as if about to lift a heavy baulk of wood.

'You don't mean him?' he questioned, pointing a blackened finger to a huge wedge of tree fixed to the workshop wall.

Above Chris's head hung a massive plank, a slice, a section of tree trunk that months earlier had been saved from the saw blades seconds before it was ripped apart. It had been rescued by Chris's father, who, seeing the words cut into it, knew immediately who had done it. Having saved it, he had supervised the keeping of it, chosen where it should be stored, and Barry had needed the help of two other men to fix it to the wall.

'Y'r mean that lad they called Maggie,' he suddenly blurted out.

'Yeah, yeah, look,' said Chris, stabbing his grimy finger at the newsprint. 'It says it 'ere.'

The two of them poured over the print as if in disbelief. They looked up at the wall, then back at the newspaper, once – twice – and again; then Barry, looking up and almost in a whisper, slowly recited the words carved into the wood. 'Where never eagle flew... Where never eagle flew.' Then they repeated it together, but this time more slowly as if in disbelief.

'Where never eagle flew.'

'I can't believe it's on our wall, the same words, here with us,' said Chris.

They now were both standing and reaching up to look more closely to make out the rest of the inscription, where the letters JM/EL were scoured inside a crudely cut heart shape, with the numbers 41 beneath.

'Well my God, who would have . . . I just thought he was . . . I can remember yer Dad tellin' me about 'im climbin' the big trees down the Lowfields and all them others int' Park. When we felled that big' un, it were yer Dad. He knew straight away when 'e read it first in t' yard. We just kept the writin' cos we couldn't believe anyone would think so much of anyone to carve it up as high as it were, like to last for ever. Now that's 'im again, and now it's in the papers.'

Chris shook his head. Pondering, he questioned himself.

'How wrong can you be, and here he was with me Dad in this yard and we never knew he was famous at writin'. He must have loved her a lot to do that . . . I wonder if he thought anyone would ever read it. . . .'

His voice trailed away as Barry reached up and brushed sawdust and cobwebs from the lower edges of this unlikely epitaph, then turned slowly on his heel towards the door to return to the saw bench.

'He must 'av bin some kind uf genius,' he ventured.

As the door closed behind him, all that Chris could do was gaze at the carved letters. Long after Barry had gone he murmured to himself.

'He was, he really was.'

Chapter 20

Cape Canaveral

The date is 28 January 1986, and space shuttle *Challenger* is ready for take-off.

This will be one of the most important days in the development of the planned exploration of outer space.

Mission control relays the launching countdown to the anticipating astronauts and to thousands of nervously waiting technicians, who have prepared every detail of this flight. There are thousands of spectators anxiously waiting behind the safety barriers, and millions of television viewers, including, by special arrangement, the nation's children. This is the day history will be made.

Mission control.

10, 9, 8, 7, 6, we have main engine start, 4, 3, 2, 1, and lift-off.
Lift-off of the 25th space shuttle mission. And it has cleared the tower.
Pilot. Roll programme.
Control. Roger, roll Challenger.
Control. Challenger go at throttle up.
Pilot. Roger go at throttle up.

It is 11.39 a.m. and *Challenger* is only 73 seconds into its flight from the launch pad at Cape Canaveral. Travelling at 2,900 feet per second, it has already crossed the Florida coastline and is 9 miles down range over the Atlantic Ocean. The dream becomes reality.

Suddenly around the fast disappearing dot in the far distance there is an orange glow, which quickly increases in size and intensity against an azure blue sky. Gasps of disbelief gush from the packed crowds of on-lookers; technicians stare in astonishment as the fireball grows and a rumbling thunder of an enormous explosion shatters the silence. The spacecraft is blown to smithereens.

The rumble of the explosion reverberates down the wind and dies. There is a stupefied silence. In a moment the dreams and aspirations of a nation have been obliterated.

Miles away in the White House in Washington, unaware of the disaster that has just occurred, President Ronald Reagan is in the Oval Office preparing his State of the Union report to Congress. He is surrounded by aides and scriptwriters eager to maximize the impact his speech will have, not only on a critical Congress, but on a nation that will be watching his every gesture and following his every word under the scrutiny of the world's television cameras. In the Oval Office there are seven men and women working at keyboards while twenty or more other aides are sorting and selecting from different documents to shape the speech's detail. This is, after all, the most important opportunity a president can ever have.

Suddenly there is commotion at one of the entrances to the room, whispers, sideways glances. The disturbance is centred on two men who officiously scan the room and head straight for the President. The first is Poindexter, the National Security Adviser, who is closely followed by Vice President Bush. The two look ashen and agitated. Poindexter closes on Reagan and clasping his hand and arm draws him close to him as he speaks. The room watches, trying to catch even one word, but the men have lowered their voices and are in close encounter. The President visibly crumbles and holds on to Poindexter; meanwhile, Bush is spreading the appalling message to others. Quickly the whole room has news of the disaster – words and desperate gestures cascade in every direction as disbelief is overcome by the horror of the brutality of the truth.

Others now push forward to surround Reagan. Amazingly among the aides there is Senator John Glen, who twenty-four years earlier had been the first American astronaut to orbit the earth. He is an associate and friend of the families of most of those men and women who are now feared dead. He himself needs comforting, but unselfishly he hides his own anguish and pain as the President turns to him for help. His voice trembles with emotion.

'Who are these men and women John, do I know them?'

Glen nods in response. He too is now visibly shaking, and a chilling silence overtakes the room as Glen reports: 'First there's Michael Smith.'

Reagan repeats the name 'Michael Smith' in a stumbling monotone.

He half closes his eyes as if trying to recall an image of the lost astronaut. The name is on the lips of every man and woman in the room. Some repeat it again and again with solemnity and disbelief without engaging with each other.

With slow deliberation Glen adds the second name.

'Dick Scobee'.

The reaction and the intoned response are repeated again and again as the remainder of the names are recalled

'Judith Resnik' – 'Judith Resnik.'

'Ronald McNair' – 'Ronald McNair.'

'Ellison Onizuka' – 'Ellison Onizuka.'

'Gregory Jarvis' – 'Gregory Jarvis.'

'Christa McAuliffe' – 'Christa McAuliffe.'

By the time the last name is given, the President is visibly bowed by the weight of the enormity of the tragedy that has engulfed not only him but his staff and the entire American nation. Shaking his head in bewilderment, he turns to those closest to him and asks: 'What the hell shall we do now?'

The question seems to be a cue to allow everyone to respond simultaneously. There are grasping hands, embraces, tears, words of comfort, but for some just blank disbelief. The noise increases moment by moment, and telephones add to the cacophony, as aides rush from one to another with little sense of order or purpose. It is chaotic.

Poindexter senses the need to bring some order to the Oval Office and, turning to the President, says, 'Ok Ron, I'll take care of this', and he moves purposefully to the centre of the developing melee. He surveys the room with an air of authority, and, as the noise subsides in anticipation, he seizes the moment. Everyone is attentive.

This unforeseen and terrible disaster will impact on every man, woman and child throughout our nation. I must ask some of you to leave us so that our President can draw round him his advisers and scriptwriters. We now need to prepare one of the most difficult speeches a President has ever had to make, guidance for our people and our nation. This speech will rightly replace the State of the Union address to Congress and we expect the transmission to go out at the same time, 1700 hours. There is no time to lose. Please stay calm, available to help if called upon, and comfort each other. We have much to do. Thank you.

Anyone caught up in a disaster looks to others, friend or family, for support and solace; but when a nation is similarly exposed, everyone turns to its leader. It is at such a time that great leadership, vision and statesmanship can console and comfort a nation.

On such occasions carefully chosen words sometimes bring new shapes and meanings to language.

In the past great leaders have chosen their words with particular care and needed considerable oratorical skills to deliver them. These occasions are rare, but those who have found appropriate words, crafted in the moment, have become icons of their time.

Reagan needed to draw upon his wealth of experience as an actor in order to capture the sentiment of this moment. The innate skills that he had successfully exercised in his career as a film star now needed to be complemented by bringing the right language together in the right order. The speech needed to be reflective and acknowledge the sacrifices made by the astronauts as of equal importance to those of great pioneers from the past. The tone must be serious but not despairing of the present, grieving but providing steadfast hope in the actions of the nation's future. It had to be humble in recognizing the sacrifices these men and women had made in the development of space exploration and acknowledge the presence of a greater order that draws all people together at such a moment.

Of the few men and women who remained surrounding the President, one woman waited, patient and composed. As others had been leaving the office, Reagan had beckoned and called her to him, and she now stood attentively close at his side. She was Peggy Noonan.

At 37 she was an alluring mixture of feminine charm and no-nonsense modesty, apparent relaxed sociability and sincere loyalty. Her clear blue eyes and girlish swirl of ash blonde hair gave no hint of the highly experienced one-time radio scriptwriter. Contracted to the Oval Office because of her exceptional talent, she had since shaped the words and sentences of every speech made by the President. He knew he could now rely on her, depend on her, to search out the appropriate words and phrases to enable him to address the American people with confidence. Within two hours, and working against the clock, she needed to turn a melee of disparate ideas from her team of advisers and scriptwriters and be ready to share a first draft script with her President.

Soon, sitting alongside him, she hands the President a sheaf of text. Reagan is fidgety as he pores over the words. As he begins the second page he seems more focused and nods as if in silent approval. The third and final page seems to trouble him and turning to Noonan he asks: 'How will we bring this all together at the end?'

'I have an idea about that Mr President,' she proffers with a reassuring smile, 'but before that, can I propose that you rehearse the text so far with us all so that we can listen to your interpretation, inflexions, pauses and intonations?'

He agrees, and slowly and deliberately intones and repeats lines and phrases until he is comfortable with the flow of the text.

Throughout the rehearsal Noonan has been not only listening but watching. Her gestures are consecutive as she smoothes, infers, interjects and shapes the form of the sounds, like an inspired conductor interpreting a score. Eventually both seem in unison, and there is consensus that the meaning and pace of the words are now both appropriate and inspirational.

Noonan then moves deliberately closer to the President, asking if she can show him some documents in private that may hold the key to the conclusion to the speech. While the others remain seated, the two of them walk to another table, where they sit together and examine documents that are in protective sleeves. Although they are reading the same single document, not a word passes between them. After several minutes of silent scrutiny, Reagan slowly turns and looks directly into her eyes.

'This', he says, 'is quite remarkable, unbelievable.'

'Yes I know,' she softly replies, her eyes moistening with the emotion of the moment.

'Where on earth did you find it?' he asks.

Slowly and carefully she responds. 'That's the extraordinary thing Mr President. It was right here in our own Congress library and it was written by an American citizen, a young pilot. I'm sure that if you felt you could read the last lines it would bring your speech to a memorable conclusion.'

Reagan stared beyond her. Now reflective, he was beginning to show that the words had stirred his emotions too. As he smudged the corner of his eye with the back of his hand, he simply said: 'I must do it. I must do it for the nation, for myself and particularly for you. But more importantly I must do it for the man who wrote it who you say sacrificed his life for our country. Tell me again. What did you say his name was?'

Peggy Noonan turned to him, smiling. For the first time she slowly and gently repeated his name.

'John Magee.'

As the last few minutes ticked away before the broadcast to the nation, the sheer professionalism of the President strengthened his resolve. He gathered himself in confident anticipation and, as the countdown reached the appointed time, he spoke.

I'd planned to speak to you tonight to report on the State of the Union. But the events of earlier today have led me to change those plans. This is a day for mourning and remembering. Nancy and I are pained to the core by the tragedy of the shuttle Challenger. We know we share this pain with all the people of our country. This is truly a national loss. Nineteen years ago almost to the day we lost three astronauts in a terrible accident on the ground. But we've never lost an astronaut in flight. We've never had a tragedy like this. And perhaps we've forgotten the courage it took for the crew of the shuttle.

But they, the Challenger seven, were aware of the dangers and overcame them and did their jobs brilliantly. We mourn seven heroes: Michael Smith, Dick Scobee, Judith Resnik, Ronald McNair, Ellison Onizuka, Gregory Jarvis and Christa McAuliffe. We mourn their loss as a nation together. To the families of the seven, we cannot bear as you do the full impact of this tragedy. But we feel the loss and we're thinking about you so very much. Your loved ones were daring and brave, and they had that special grace, that special spirit that says, give me a challenge and I'll meet it with joy. They had a hunger to explore the universe and discover its truths. They wished to serve and they did. They served all of us. We've grown used to wonders in this century. It's hard to dazzle us. But for 25 years the United States space program has been doing just that. We've grown used to the idea of space and perhaps we forget that we've only just begun. We're still pioneers. They, the members of the Challenger crew, were pioneers.

And I want to say something to the school children of America who were watching the live coverage of the shuttle's take-off. I know it's hard to understand, but sometimes painful things like this happen. It's all part of the process of exploration and discovery. It's all part of taking a chance and expanding man's horizons. The future doesn't belong to the faint hearted. It belongs to the brave. The Challenger crew was pulling us into the future and we'll continue to follow them. I've always had great faith in and respect for our space program. And what happened today does nothing to diminish it. We don't hide our space program. We don't keep secrets and cover things up. We do it all up front and in public. That's the way freedom is and we wouldn't change it for a minute. We'll continue our quest in space. There will be more shuttle flights and more shuttle crews, and, yes, more volunteers, more civilians, more teachers in space. Nothing ends here. Our hopes and our journeys continue.

I want to add that I wish I could talk to every man and woman who works for NASA or who worked on this mission, and tell them your dedication and professionalism have moved and impressed us for decades and we know of your anguish. We share it.

There's a coincidence today. On this date 390 years ago, the great explorer Sir Francis Drake died aboard ship off the coast of Panama. In his lifetime, the great frontiers were the oceans, and a historian later said, 'He lived by the sea, died on it and was buried in it.' Well, today, we can say of the Challenger crew, their dedication was, like Drake's, complete. The crew of the space shuttle Challenger honoured us with the manner in which they lived their lives. We will never forget them or the last time we saw them, this morning, as they prepared for their journey and waved goodbye. They 'slipped the surly bonds of Earth to touch the face of God'. Thank you.

Newspapers across America carried a full transcription of the speech the next day.

A photograph of a tight-lipped President Reagan taken after his address complemented many of the reports that together were telegraphed around the world to millions of people who had not only been horrified by the tragedy but moved by the content and message of the address. The speech had not only encapsulated the feelings and thoughts of a nation but had crossed continents.

So in a moment John Magee's message in those carefully crafted and inspired words had encompassed the world.

Poems published by John Magee in 1939

The following poems were published by John Magee in 1939. He was just 17 years old and studying at the Avon Old Farms School, near Hartford, Connecticut in the United States of America. The book was dedicated to E.B.L., Elinor Lyon, who was the daughter of Hugh Lyon, the head-master of Rugby Public School in England, where John studied from 1935 to 1939. He wrote in the copy he sent her 'To Elinor from a nostalgic John, Dec 1939.' The poem by which John is now known throughout the world, 'High Flight', was later added to Elinor's copy of the book where she also wrote her own recollections of John in the emotive poem dedicated to him 'J.G.M.' in 1943.

The Latin inscription *Forsan et haec olim meminisse iuvabit* can be translated as 'Perhaps we will delight in remembering times past'.

John Magee's Foreword to the 1939 book of poems:

> This little book is thrust upon the world, not as being in any sense
> a work of art, but rather as a potential object of interest for those of
> sufficient curiosity to read it; and the sole reason for the publication
> of these immature verses is that they may possibly be acceptable
> to the more indulgent as representing various emotional conflicts
> occurring in the life of a boy between the ages of thirteen and
> sixteen, and that they may, perhaps, bring back to the reader, if
> readers there be, something of his or her own youth, when Wonder
> was fighting for life in the teeth of Pride, and Love lay shivering
> under the howling winds of adolescent Cynicism.
>
> The fact that I printed them myself, with the invaluable help and
> advice of Mr. Max Stein, will, I hope, be no great impediment to
> their acceptability. However, all I ask is that they be read not too

critically, and that they be permitted by the Muses to give some pleasure to my contemporaries, but more particularly to those for whom Youth is but a laughing ghost of the Long Ago. ...

Lines Written on a Sleepless Night

I love the moon's soft mist-encircled light;
It weaves a silver spell; the very leaves
Seem turned to silver-stone! – surely tonight
There's something strange abroad! Beneath the eaves
Thrushes are nestling, – hushed; and these I love;
And, too, I love thin spires of smoke, that rise
Like incense to the stars; and then, to move
When all the world's asleep, or to surprise
A wakeful mouse from some close hiding place...
I love to think I hear an angel's voice
Hung on the whisper of the wind. This place,
This night, this hour, this sky, are all my choice!
I love the earth, the sea, the heaven above,
But, more than these, the right to say I love!

Sonnet after Catullus:
Vivamus, mea Lesbia, atque amemus . . .

Sweetheart, to live a life of careless love,
Unharried by the vapidness of Age!
– To live, whether there's sun or moon above
Content, within a lover's tutelage;
To share the dreams of every tranquil night;
Ask nothing more than someone to adore;
So while we live, let kisses bring delight –
Kiss me a thousand times, – a hundred more,
Again a thousand; may we never tire
Of showing outward signs of inward Love
To cool the burning flame of our desire!
And then, lest any envier reprove,
We'll start again, no matter what the score,
– And lip to lip we'll kiss for evermore!

Song of the Dead

A Reproach to this Century

Also our lives were tragic; we believed
In the earth, heavy beneath us, trusted the sun
As it played on leaves and flowers, and we conceived
Truth, and True Beauty, – End of Things Begun;
We, too, have laughed, and sung our hundred songs
The sons we bore were perfect in our eyes
We called them Brave, Original, and Wise;
We saw them slain, with faith we bore our wrongs
Watched we the clouds, – and did not understand
– Longed, too, for happiness; and knew despair,
Lay with our dreams in the gutters, and were deceived
By eyes of women; whispered hand in hand –
And loved the moonlight on a lover's hair –
We were but a day in Eternity, – yet we believed. ...

Sonnet to Rupert Brooke

We laid him in a cool and shadowed grove
One evening, in the dreamy scent of time,
Where leaves were green, and whispered high above
– A grave as humble as it was sublime;
There, dreaming in the fading deeps of light –
The hands that thrilled to touch a woman's hair;
Brown eyes, that loved the Day, and looked on Night,
A soul that found at last its answered prayer. …

There daylight, as a dust, slips through the trees,
And drifting, gilds the fern about his grave –
Where even now, perhaps, the evening breeze
Steals shyly past the tomb of him who gave
New sight to blinded eyes; who sometimes wept –
A short time dearly loved; and after, – slept.

Sonnet

Si bene quid de te merui, fuit aut tibi quicquam
Dulce meum. ...

If, when we walked together in the rain,
While tears and raindrops mingled in our eyes;
And talked of foolish things, to ease the pain
Of parting; when we thought we could disguise
Our feelings in the light of stolen joy;
When fawning bracken kissed our sodden shoes,
And hand in hand, determined to enjoy
Those last few moments we were soon to lose,
We walked in silence, awed by shrouding mist
And wondered at that silent wilderness
Of moor and mountain, and the pall above,
And laughed awhile, – and sometimes all but kissed;
If then we found a little happiness,
Did neither of us see that this was – Love?

No. 9 Elementary Flying Training School, St Catharine's, Ontario, 15 February 1941. Left to right, Fred Heather, Tom Gain, Duncan Fowler, John Magee. *All pictures in this section are from a private collection unless credited otherwise.*

John Magee, during pilot training in Canada.

John Magee stands far left during pilot training in Canada.

John Magee as a new member of the Royal Canadian Air Force, Ontario, 1940.

(See image below for caption). *Ivan Henson Collection*

Uplands, Ottawa, No. 2 Service Flying Training School. The commander, Group Captain Wilf Curtis presents John with his pilot's Wings brevet, 16 June 1941. *Collection of Manuscript Division of the Library of Congress*

(Left) Royal Canadian Air Force pilot John Magee. (Below) A series of portraits of Pilot Officer John Magee from a 1941 contact sheet.

'Stranded in Iceland' in transit to the UK. From left to right Hughie Russell, not known, George 'Terk' Bayley, Jack Coleman, John Magee.

No. 53 Operational Training Unit, No. 7 Course, Llandow, Wales, 1941. John Magee is third row up, third from left. *Coleman Collection*

John Magee on the right with Jack Coleman outside the dispersal hut on Wellingore airfield, late 1941.

John Magee outside the dispersal hut at Wellingore, 1941.

John Magee at Wellingore.

Hart Massey. Intelligence Officer No. 412
Squadron, Wellingore.

Hart Massey's father on a diplomatic exchange
inspecting aircraft at Wellingore.

John Magee, next to 'Brunhilde' at Wellingore.

Rod Smith, left, and Dusty Davidson at the dispersal hut at Wellingore airfield, 1941.

Crashed 412 Squadron Spitfire, 1941.

John Magee in Spitfires at Wellingore.

His Majesty King George VI inspects No. 412 Squadron, November 1941.

His Majesty King George VI, inside a dispersal hut at Wellingore airfield, November 1941.

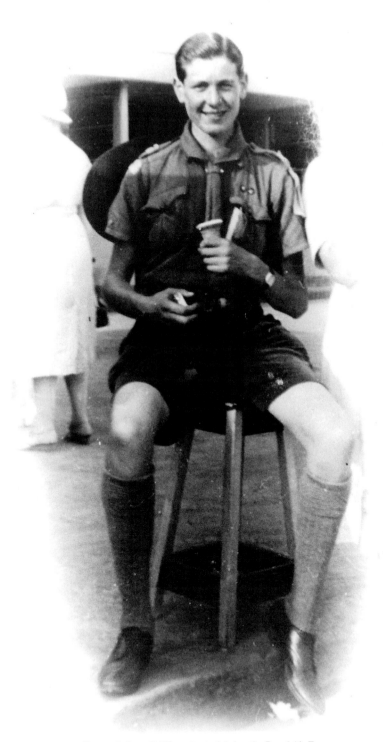

Ernest Aubrey Griffin prior to joining the Royal Air Force.

Leading Aircraftman Ernest Aubrey Griffin, who lost his life in the collision of 11 December 1941.

Initial cross at Scopwick Church burial ground, marking the grave of John Magee. This is the photograph the Magee family received soon after their son's death.

Left to right, Ivan Henson, Hart Massey, unknown and Rod Smith at RAF Digby, 1982.

Scopwick Church burial ground, Lincolnshire. The permanent headstone of Pilot Officer J. G. Magee, who lost his life on 11 December 1941, aged 19. *Fighting High*

To a Drowned Friend

Sunt lacrimae rerum et morten mortalia targunt

Black rocks, foam-crowned, raise
Their darkling heads from circling waves
High-pinnacled, like towered maze
Of some old castle. Silent, they lure
The helpless craft; while, olivine, the sea
(The quandary alike of high and low)
In silent fury clutches frantically
The air, in vain appeal. Far below,
Deep in his long green bosom, lies
My friend. Contented, he sleeps
Through green glooms in darkness absolute,
In those eternal hyaline deeps.
Alas! My friend, whom once I loved;
But shall I never see thee more
'Till grey waves cease to beat their frantic arms
Along the shore?

To Persephone
(First attempt October 1938)

Oh! How to soothe my numbly-aching heart?
– How while away the pain that shattered joy
Leaves ever in its path? – At every start
Of hope, it seems that something in the boy
Is doomed to die! Oft in my waking dreams
I find your face; you smile; you beckon; – taunt
Me with sweet joys that cheat my soul, and flaunt
Your very self before my eyes; it seems
That Love is Hell! But must I always bear
The pain of Love? – And is it but in vain
To breathe out sonnets to the midnight air,
To long to touch your lustrous hair again?
I thought to find some joy in 'Life's Sweet Breath'
But what remains in Life, if Life is Death?

Elissa
(Second attempt)

Oh! How to soothe my numbly-aching heart?
How while away the pain that truant joy
Leaves in its vacant room? At every start
Of hope, it seems that something in the boy
Is doomed to die! Oft in my making dreams
I find your face; you smile; you beckon; – taunt
Me with sweet joys that cheat my soul, and flaunt
Your lovely self before my eyes. It seems
To love is pain! But must I always bear
The pain of Love? And is it but in vain
To breathe out sonnets to the midnight air,
To long to touch your lips, your hair, again?
I thought to find new joy with every breath,
But what remains, if Life alone is Death?

I Thought to Find

I thought to find
Glory, fighting,
Long struggles with men,
With one man smiting
Another; the smell
Of sweat; the soldier-pain
Of effort; that, after,
There would be rest, – and laughter.

But what I found was Mangled me biting
A heathen dust, and ground
Strewn with heads and
Eyes, and twisted hands,
Holding nothing.
God! Why is it that no one understands
The meaning of
FUTILITY?
– They would, had they but seen
– Horrible, staring eyes …

No Title
– written on RCAF paper and almost certainly when on guard duty.

Slowly the night goes, slowly
And, silent, the listening stars
Hear only the tramp of the sentry,
And occasional passing cars.

Out over the field there is silence,
Where battle planes rest on the earth,
On the land which affords them respite
From the trials that assail them from birth.

No Title
*– written on RCAF paper and probably written
in Canada in 1940/41.*

Just now I felt your lovely body shaking
As you gave your lips to mine to say goodnight.
As a child trembles on a sudden waking
Fearing the unseen darkness, craving light.
And suddenly I knew that you were frightened
Of the time when vision goes, and colour dies.
And then my eager hands around you tightened,
For I knew that life of mine was in your eyes.

Heart! If the time must come, let's meet it bravely,
And not with sadness, but to glory fanned
By thoughts of those who made the journey safely,
– So stepping quietly from the shades of strife
With laughter on our lips, and hand in hand
– Kneel at the altar of eternal life.

Dawn

Darkness … stars overhead
Silent in clear rotation,
Silent in expectation,
Waiting for the dawn …

Twilight … grey in the East,
Glittering stars on the wane;
The world, and a quiet lane
Slumbering on …

Slowly, New Dawn creeps in,
Changing in phantasmal hues;
Watching, the world imbues
Another morn …

Suddenly, birds are singing,
Welcoming Dawn in all her Glory,
Telling the age-old wonder-story
Once again.

Pork Pie

From Switzerland, you say?
I think the Swiss have finer, greyer hats, and, in them, preen
Themselves on lonely Alps. But this,
This was a most intolerable green!

Do you remember how I tried to toss,
The hated object down a waterfall,
And lost it among the moss?
What made you buy that awful hat at all?

Besides, you wore it daily; once appeared
Wearing the thing in London – then I tried
To feed the thing to Mike, who clearly feared
Canine regurgitations from inside.

And yet, I can remember, when we parted
You wore it, as you beamed a last farewell;
And soon I realized – but how it smarted!
I loved the damn thing more than words can tell. ...

Lines for the Newly Dead

These, too, had thought of angels; felt the wheeling
Dizziness of space, and sweep of wings;
Who also wept for pain, – and knew the healing
Gladness of children; fingered tiny things;
Yearned, too, for vengeance, knew the throbbing flood
Of anger round the brain; considered slaughter;
These loved rich coils of morning smoke; saw blood;
– And found the cool oblivion of water ...

Darkness was theirs, and night winds; lazy laughter;
and fear; – the windy eagerness of sails
Slanting the ocean; these had heard the tread
Of Death upon the stair, – and shortly after,
A distant train's faint thunder on the rails –
These, too, had thought of angels ... and are dead!

Entry Of The Heroes*

But who are these who enter one by one
The darkened halls, their passive labours done?
– Who these black minions, – though with Youth endowed,
Who file within, a pale plebeian crowd?
Are these the servants of a loftier race?
And why this torpid stare on every face?
The silent, awestruck throng grows thick, until
The waking buildings soon begin to fill
With shadowy, stooping forms; they take their place
In ordered rows, a sombre populace.
Now all is silent, and a breathless hush
Awaits the advent throng; a golden flush
Illumes the portal designate; all eyes
Embrace the door to obviate surprise …

The organ-trump sends up a regal note;
'The Heroes come!' – the cry in every throat
Unspoken. Then, in glory unsurpassed
They enter, each more splendid than the last.
To lead the throng comes Paris, aged lord,
In sisters rich, but hesitant of word.
Achilles next – he struts with kingly gait;
His crested plumelets nod, importunate,
As if to ape his motions, he whose trade
Consists of voicing endless, dull, tirade;
What care is this we see upon his brow,

– Or has this frown become ingrained now?
Him do his fawning sycophants beguile,
For seldom do they see Achilles smile.
Then Memnon comes, in volume infinite,
For Law and Order caring not a whit;
Among these minions sits his only son,
But who, from out the swart, may find the one?
Next Ajax, of the bright proboscid pink,
Ascribed by some to choler, some to drink;
A vermeil cape refulgent on his back,
To toilers kind – a terror to the slack.
Then wide-eyed Jason, sunken at the cheek,
His unctuous locks brushed smooth, his gaze oblique.
But whose this hirsute countenance severe,
– A second Esau, horrent at the ear?
Then comes Apollo, scholar laureate;
In accent strange – in figure – adequate,
With Mars, his truckling in the same pursuit
(though epidermically destitute).
Then Perseus comes, in lucent robes bedight,
Of martial fame, subordinate in height.
He leads the Arm of Youth to victory,
– His air more apt than his ability.
And last of all Orion, he whose ear
Has suffered from a pugilist career.

The Forest*

Midnight –
How still is the world tonight!
A forest lies ahead, sunk in slumber;
From its shadowy depth
No voice
Calls me to welcome me. Must I step
From the soft moon's silvered light
Into eternal night?

I entered.
At once I was aware of life, and yet
No sound I heard. Something
Brushed my face. My straining ears
Caught nothing. As I walked
I seemed to move further
And further
From Life. Death
Beckoned, drawing me ever onward
Into its gaping bosom;
The trees
Mocked me, – faces gnarled and lichened
Leered derision, pointing their long, thin fingers
Towards the End;
– the End … and then …?
I stooped.
Deep silence

Filled my ears, my nose, my throat,
Choking me ...
I felt my brow; my eyes
Were filled with sweat. I turned
And, turning, ran stumbling blindly
Through the forest. Fear
Was at my heels.
I had no eyes for leering trees
And pointing fingers. My knees
Began to sag, and I could see no light;
Fear, Life's greatest Hustler, drove me on.
I fought for breath. I tried to shout.
No answer met my troubled call
But that of Echo – still I could see no light.
Fainting, I prayed: –
'Oh God!' ... and then
I saw the moon ... I ran ...

I stopped, and raised my head.
The moon
Smiled down at me. I looked
At the forest, peaceful now
And wondered at my foolishness.

De Corpore

Frequently I have thought of the startling beauty of women,
Calling to mind the glad mouth, and the nose and eyes,
And the plaintive fallings of hair upon shoulders, and instantly
I have thought that no other thing is so beautiful.

I too, have known the fond, swift, momentary passion
(Leaving a tickling hotness in the palm of the hand, thrilling
the groin)
Of knees beneath pleated skirts in the throbbing of [?]
And feel the desire for holding – for utter possession.
(Knowing the while that no other beauty is comparable).

No Title

... are stars that beautify this night,
I call my soul. Laughing across the years,
They thrill again my memory, as light
Falls over hills at dawn; and through the tears.

I seem to see you standing, where we parted;
White as a petal, on a winter's day,
I tried to fight the sudden tears that started
– You leaned, and lingered; then you turned away ...

Then we were happy, wandered hand in hand
Through life, when all we had was Love, and Youth.
– Till you had gone, I did not understand
That your glad eyes were loveliness, and Truth!

[It is believed this was submitted to the editors of
The New Rugbeian, *because the word 'still' has been
added between the words 'that' and 'beautify' in line one.
And all of the third verse is crossed out.]*

No Title

I thought your mouth as lovely
As wind knows peach-tree blossom in Cathay
Dreaming slow-perfumed under the stars, and forever
In Eastern tapestries – lips, waiting patiently
As petals never stirring until the first
Sleep-stirring breeze that comes from beyond the mountains.

*[This attempt, lacking some punctuation, is believed to have
been submitted to the editors of* The New Rugbeian. *
The following comments appear beneath: 'Gives a feeling
of wonderment and ecstasy – almost awe. Sort of hazy
and voluptuous. The impression it makes is hard to explain.
I like it.']*

The Cowboy

I'm leavin' my house, and I'm quittin' my home,
And I'm thinkin' it's all for the best;
I'm loadin' my pack-horse, I'm cleanin' my gun,
– For I'm takin' the road to the West.

I'm greasin' my saddle, I'm shinin' my spurs,
I'm feelin' the need of a change;
I'm sick of the life in this dirty ole town,
So I'm ridin' the Western Range.

So farewell, ole homestead, – so long, ole dawg,
I'll be seein' you later, I guess;
For I'm making my start in a new Wanderlust,
 – And I'm ridin' the Trail to the West.

Hints for Conscriptiai
(to prevent people of either class from offending
each other's sensibilities)

I. The Over-Educated.
Don't imagine that you're still a Sergeant in the Corps;
You're not a better soldier, though you know a little more.
Don't smoke Havanas, when you know that 'Weights' 'll do,
Or drink Dry Martini, when your beer 'll get you through.
Don't talk of Rugby, and the prizes that you won;
– He's just as proud of you, because he's Father's Only Son!

II. The Under-Educated.
Don't laugh at Cholmondly 'cos he's got a funny name,
And even if he washes, he's a fellow just the same;
Don't think he's superior, because he wears a hat,
Or [?] him when he says his prayers – he's used to doing that –
Always respect him whatever you do,
Remember that he's probably as much respect for you!

Pops

I write in praise of Burton's Pops,
Of frothing bottles, seething cups;
Of luscious flavours, brimming full,
And tempting you to take a 'pull'.

For why, I ask, do men drink beer,
And whisky, causing drunken leer?
I hold that Pops are just as nice
As any alcoholic vice.

Though Bacchus was the God of Wine,
And Dionysus found the vine;
The wine they drank was not the same
As that which Moderns term Champagne!

Oh! Would that I were a millionaire!
– I would not simply walk on air;
I'd make my way towards a shop,
– And buy myself – an Orange Pop!

And so, I say, drink Pops for Health;
Drink Pops for Wisdom, Strength, and Wealth;
For Happiness, for everything;
– And so to bed, – God Save the King!

Bibliography

Falconer, Jonathan. *Life as a Battle of Britain Pilot*. Sutton Publishing: 2007.

Garnett, Stephen. *The Complete Works of John Magee, The Pilot Poet*. This England Books: 1989.

Garnett, Stephen. *A Tribute to John Magee. The Pilot Poet*. This England Books: 1982.

Garnett, Stephen. *Salute to the Soldier Poets*. This England Books: 1990.

Hagedorn, Hermann. *Sunward I've Climbed: The Story of John Magee, Poet and Soldier 1922–1941*. The Macmillan Co.: 1944.

Lucas, Laddie. *Thanks for the Memory*. Grub Street: 1998.

Lyon, Hugh. *A Memoir*. Privately Published: 1993.

Magee, John. *Collected Poems*. Avon Old Farms Press: 1939.

Magee, John. *Collected Poems*. Facsimile edition with additions, Cumberland Galleries: 2012.

Otter, Patrick. *Lincolnshire Airfields in the Second World War*. Countryside Books: 1996.

Rennison, John. *The Digby Diary*. Aspect Publishing: 2003.

Unpublished Sources

Royal Canadian Air Force, Pilot's Flying Log Book of John Gillespie
Magee. Author's collection.
Royal Canadian Air Force, Public Archives, Canada, Officer
Application and Record – 4/7/1941.
Royal Canadian Air Force Special Reserve, Record of Service
Airmen – 22/6/1941.
Statement of Service – 21/5/1986.
Royal Canadian Air Force, Operations Record Book No. 412
Squadron. Copy 1991. Author's collection.
Rugby School Records, – May 1936 April 1936, Oxford and
Cambridge Examination Board. Credit passes in seven subjects.
Royal Air Force College, Cranwell Lincolnshire, Operations Record
Book, December 1941.
Death Certificate of Aubrey Griffin – 19/12/1941.

The Magee and Backhouse family histories. Private collection.
The Ivan Henson Archive. Private collection.
Recorded interview author with Elinor Wright. Private collection.
Letters to and from Norman Griffin – 18/6/1991. Private collection.
Copies of letters to and from Mrs E. Griffin and Reverend. J. Magee
February and March 1942. Private collection.

Notes

1   Ideally the fence should be set back a distance of thirty-five times the height of the fence. The snow fence forces the wind to go around and through it, thereby causing it to lose speed and energy. Suspended snow particles drop out as the wind speed decreases, forming drifts in front of and behind the fence. (Snow Fence Guide. Strategic Highway Research Programme. Iowa Department of Transport.)

2   Since 1485, Ireland, with its largely Roman Catholic population, had been under the domination of Protestant England. But by the early eighteenth century even the Irish Protestant minority had begun to resent the political and economic domination of English interests. From 1775 the Irish nation had watched in disbelief as colonies in America had joined together to break free from the British Empire. The Revolution had a profound effect in Ireland and furthered reason to challenge the British Government's dominance of the Irish people, exemplified, for example, by its procurement of Irish troops for the war with the American colonies. Consequently a gradual disassociation began among Anglicans, Protestants and Roman Catholics. By 1783 a total sympathy for the American revolutionaries had developed, since they had succeeded in their quest for independence in a way in which the Irish had not. Almost all Irishmen now looked admiringly and longingly across the Atlantic to America and were determined to escape their harsh economic and religious control and find the 'promised land'. So in 1788 Robert Magee joined thousands of other Irish men and women and emigrated with his family to the United States of America. Robert Magee so became the progenitor of the Magees of Pittsburgh.

3   The house now known as Pinewood House was built right on the
     cliff top with dramatic views over the English Channel.

4   Dermott's diary.

5   Dermott's diary.

6   Dermott's diary.

7   Letter from John Magee to Douglas Eves, 28 March 1940.

8   Letter from John Magee to Douglas Eves, 28 March 1940.

9   The first outward signs to the world of unrest between China and
     Japan occurred early 1932 when Japan declared Manchuria
     independent. By the summer of that year the political thuggery of
     the Nazi Party had established the power base for Hitler to be
     elected as Chancellor of Germany. Even at that time omens of a
     world upheaval 'warfare' cannot have escaped John's father as a
     missionary in China. With both himself, his wife and young family
     in one of the most vulnerable parts of the world, it is not
     surprising that he sent them to England for safety.

10   Letter from John to his father, August 1940.

11   Letter from Harvard, June 1940, offers scholarship. Letter from
     Yale, 17 July 1940, offers interview and scholarship.

12   Letter from Uncle Jim, May 1940.

13   Draft of a letter sent to the Secretary of War, 16 August 1940, only
     weeks before John crossed over the border into Canada to join
     the RCAF.

14   Reverend John Magee to America on 9 June 1940.

15   Letter to Christopher Magee, July 1941.

16   Letter from Reverend John Magee to Charles Seymour,
     16 September 1940.

17   Letters in this chapter are from John Magee to his family.

18   His log book shows it was 6.5 hours.

19   Alan Stinton obtained his pilot's licence in January 1939 and was
     'recruited' in that autumn by RCAF to become an instructor.

20   Letter to Ivan Henson, 2 October 1969.

21   This incident is identified by John in his log book with the now
     customary exclamation mark, and Squadron Leader Wilmot
     wrote: 'Aircraft ground looped, assessed as inexperience.'

22   Ivan Henson collection – from a relative of F/O Paterson.

23   Letter from John Magee to his father, 16 June 1941.

24 Letter from John Magee to his family.

25 The *California* was an Anchor Line liner launched on 17 April 1923, weighing 16,792 tons and 575 feet long. She was requisitioned by the Admiralty on 25 August 1939 and sank on 11 July 1943.

26 Letter from John Magee to his parents, date had been censored.

27 Letter from John Magee to his family.

28 Letter from John Magee to his parents, date had been censored.

29 Letter from John Magee to his family.

30 Mick Wilson and his wife Jeane, known as Jeaney, lived on the station at Llandow. Jeaney, a nurse, looked after John for several days in the sick bay in mid-September. Together they knew John to be a 'man apart who could quote famous writers and poets'. Interview 2012.

31 Letter from John Magee to his family.

32 While John was at Uplands, sequences for this film were made where John, together with other trainees, flew Harvard trainers. James Cagney starred in the production.

33 Letter from John Magee to his family.

34 Tanya Davis, Phyllie, and a third girl, who wished only to be known as Mimi, but who has always claimed that he asked her to marry him.

35 Spencer's Wood, near Reading.

36 Author's interview with Elinor.

37 Letter to family. It was here that he first met Pilot Officer Rod Smith, who was also 19 years old. It quickly transpired that Rod had also trained at Uplands and crossed the Atlantic in the *California*, arriving at Uxbridge in England on 2 May 1941.

38 His log book identifies this aircraft as Spitfire R6612 Mark 1-14 October.

39 His log book also describes the problems as 'U/C trouble and cowlings blew loose 14 October'.

40 Log book entry, 17 October: 'A/C test – E.M. Panel blew out. Cowlings loose and U/C trouble.'

41 Letter to family.

42 Wellingore airfield was known by Code WC1, Coleby airfield WC2 and Digby airfield and base WC.

43 Wellingore Hall was built in 1760 in the Palladian style. It was enlarged in 1800 and again in 1870 to the designs and plans of John MacVicar Anderson (1835–1915).

44 This account was written by Charles Durrett, who was posted from RAF Cranwell to Digby in 1941 as a Liaison Officer between flying squadrons and contractors.

45 Interview with Elinor, 2006. Elinor had gone up to Oxford in the autumn of 1941.

46 The opera was written by Peter Blackmore and first released in 1941.

47 When asked about this comment years later, Elinor laughed and said: 'He said he didn't know if it was deliberate – of course it was. He had come to see me', emphasizing the 'me'.

48 Letter from John Magee to his parents.

49 Peter Wright married Elinor in 1944. He was in the RAF; she gave up Oxford to help in the war effort and became a radio operator in the WRNS. He returned to teaching after the war, and they had four children.

50 From the collection of E. S. Love. Permission to publish granted through courtesy of Mrs M. M. Waggoner, recipient of the original from the author in 1941.

51 Brunhilde, sometimes spelt Brynhild, was one of the valkyries in the nineteenth-century opera *Der Ring des Nibelungen* written by the German composer Richard Wagner.

52 Rod Smith's account of this accident was that 'he let his wing drop on landing and caused it damage. He was so distraught at his mistake that he taxied into a parked aircraft, hitting one of its wing tips with his own. His Flight Commander, Christopher Bushell, known as Kit and soon to become our CO, was not amused.' Ivan Henson private papers.

53 Completed on 3 December 1941, this letter was held up by censorship and did not arrive in Washington until 2 March 1942.

54 Still there today.

55 Rod Smith, 'The next day the Daily Mirror had a photo taking up to half to two thirds of its front page.' Ivan Henson private papers.

56 Hart Massey, the Wellingore Squadron's Intelligence Officer, was older than most of the pilots. Before the war he had been at Oxford University and, because of his underdeveloped physique,

he had won a place as cox in the Oxford/Cambridge Boat Race. 'Earlier that morning a dispatch rider had arrived with a package containing China tea and a lemon and he also brought a signal telling us that we would be receiving a visitor from an important place' and we were to 'serve him China tea with lemon'. Ivan Henson papers.

57 Interview with author, 2004.

58 Quote attributed to Abraham Lincoln. A favourite phrase of John Coleman from letter and conversations with sister and family in Ivan Henson papers.

59 Hart Massey had studied History at Balliol College, Oxford, and had been cox in the University Boat Race in 1939. Physically he was ideally suited to be the cox to a rowing eight, since he was light in weight and small in stature, under 5 feet tall. As a child, he had been seriously ill and was diagnosed to have a rare disease known as Rathke's pouch, a tumour that develops in the area of the brain called the hypothalamus, close to the pituitary gland. Its medical name is craniopharyngioma (cranio – skull; pharynx – throat; oma – tumour).

60 Hart Massey recalls: 'I was commissioned in the RCAF in October 1939 and, except for a brief posting to 242 Squadron at Church Fenton, served as an Intelligence Officer in RAF HQ London until the fall of 1941, when I was posted to 412 Squadron at Digby and Wellingore. My father, as Intelligence Officer, was Canada's first minister in Washington and served as Canadian High Commissioner in London during the war years and was the first Canadian to hold the office of Governor General of Canada.' Ivan Henson papers.

61 Later Rod Smith recalled that there were three or four other incidents of passengers in Spitfires – one or two fatal – and one court martial. Jack Morrison, he recalled, found out, but did nothing about it.

62 Recollections of Hart Massey, 1974. Ivan Henson papers.

63 Part of John's 'Brave New World' poem written at 16. It was written at Rugby School in 1939, for which he was awarded the Rupert Brooke Poetry Prize; Rupert Brooke had been a pupil at Rugby School thirty-five years earlier.

64 Sergeant Powell was flying a Spitfire Vb AD349. He escaped with minor injuries, but the aircraft was a total wreck.

65 Letter from John Magee to Dermott, 8 December 1941.

66 Letter from Rod Smith, April 1987. Ivan Henson papers.

67 Extracts from notes and letters from Jim Hartland to the author.

68 The swimming pool and its surrounding buildings were known as 'The Tosh'.

69 Privately printed. Avon Old Farms Press, 1939.

Index